# THE ULTIMATE
# RACING CAR
## BOOK

# THE ULTIMATE
# RACING CAR
## BOOK

*David Burgess-Wise*

**DK**

## DORLING KINDERSLEY
LONDON · NEW YORK · SYDNEY · MOSCOW
www.dk.com

**DK**

## A DORLING KINDERSLEY BOOK

Visit us on the World Wide Web
at www.dk.com

**Editor** Teresa Pritlove
**Project Art Editor** Philip J. Ormerod
**Senior Managing Editor** Martyn Page
**Senior Managing Art Editor** Bryn Walls
**Production** Silvia La Greca
**Picture Research** Cynthia Frazer

Designed and Typeset by
THE BRIDGEWATER BOOK COMPANY LIMITED
**Senior Designer** Kevin Knight
**Designer** Chris Akroyd

First published in 1999 by Dorling Kindersley Limited,
9 Henrietta Street, London, WC2E 8PS

2 4 6 8 10 9 7 5 3 1

Copyright © 1999 Dorling Kindersley Limited, London
Text copyright © 1999 David Burgess-Wise

A CIP catalogue record for this book is available from
the British Library

ISBN 0 7513 0662 2

Colour reproduction by GRB Editrice, Verona, Italy

Printed and bound in Hong Kong by Dai Nippon

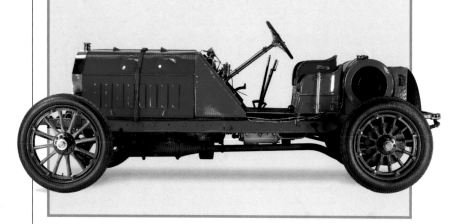

# Contents

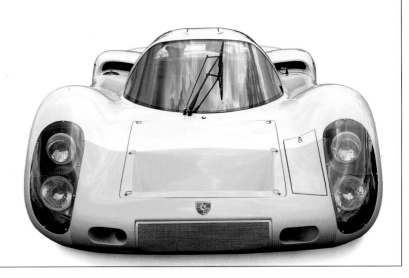

# Author's preface

MOTOR RACING and its history have fascinated me for as long as I can remember. At the end of the 1950s, when Brooklands, the world's first purpose-built race track, was still part of the Vickers Aircraft works and off limits to the public, a friend and I parked near the old access road and scrambled up onto the weed-grown Members' Banking. Breathless, we stood there on the steeply cambered concrete savouring the atmosphere.

A few years later, I interviewed some of the drivers who had raced at Brooklands, and saw some of the cars from those golden days in action. Later still, I played a very small part in the establishment of a permanent museum on the Brooklands site, which is fascinating even to those of us who were not born when racing ceased there.

The combination of the skill and daring of the drivers with the mechanical genius of the men who build their machines makes motor racing a heady cocktail. I count myself fortunate to have met some of the great names of motor racing over the years, including Juan Fangio – possibly the greatest ever.

I have also been lucky enough to drive some of the legendary cars from racing history, which only reinforces my admiration for their drivers and designers. I hope that I have been able to communicate some of my enthusiasm for these fine machines in these pages.

DAVID BURGESS-WISE

▼ **AMERICAN LEGEND**

The Kurtis-Offenhauser was one of the most successful, and colourful, postwar racing cars to appear at Indianapolis.

# Foreword

WHEN David Burgess-Wise showed me a proof copy of *The Ultimate Racing Car Book*, I was most impressed by the range and photographic clarity of the hundreds of images of memorable racing cars. I am fortunate that my own racing career gave me the chance to drive some of the fabulous cars featured in this book, including the now-legendary Mercedes-Benz 300SLR. It also gave me the opportunity to compete with, and know as friends, some great drivers. Reading about their careers in the book's Racing Personalities section brought back many fond memories.

I am lucky enough still to be able to drive some of the exciting cars that I raced in my youth in retrospective events, which have now become an integral part of the motor-racing calendar. Many of today's racing enthusiasts display a profound interest in the history of the sport. *The Ultimate Racing Car Book* should appeal to them as it celebrates the evolution of motor racing, with each generation meeting new challenges and producing new heroes.

Over 50 years ago, I remember glancing admiringly at Raymond Mays' 2-litre ERA – a veteran even then – and being inspired by that car. I, in turn, hope that the cars featured in this book will inspire a new generation of drivers. Motor racing, even after a hundred years, remains the world's most exciting sport.

STIRLING MOSS

# THE HISTORY OF RACING

# 1

It began with one man and a car racing against the clock, and developed into an international sport that has never ceased to excite and fascinate. From the thunderous machines that raced from city to city in the early days of the motoring age to today's sleek Grand Prix projectiles, there runs an unbroken history that combines triumph and tragedy, skill and chance, advanced technology and the art of the engine tuner. The history of motor racing is as enthralling as any fictional adventure: there have been numerous situations in which the underdog has finally triumphed because of sheer ability and superior car preparation. After a century of competition, motor sport is more popular than ever, with a worldwide following that has reached the millions. This chapter covers some of the milestones in the history of motor sports, depicting the human urgency to improve on design and technique in the unceasing quest for speed.

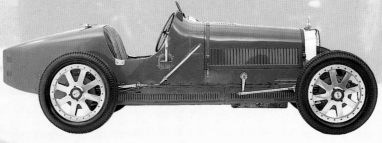

# THE HISTORY OF RACING

Racing, it is said, improves the road-going breed. That may or may not be true. What is certainly true is that motor racing has brought enjoyment – and excitement – to millions of people. It supports a successful and highly skilled industry and has certainly accelerated the development of the motor car, which has changed more in a century than the horse has in a millennium.

The world's first racing car, a little steam quadricycle built by the Parisian firm of De Dion, Bouton, & Trépardoux in 1884, had very little in common with modern racing cars. Instead of a bonnet, it had a round, upright boiler; the control panel was limited to a few pressure gauges and sight glasses on the boiler; and there was no steering-wheel but, instead, a spade handle by the side of the body to guide the vehicle. The twin-cylinder steam engine generated a top speed of 56 kph (35 mph), which was faster than any other mode of transport in the 1880s except the railway train. However, the quadricycle lacked opposition, and when it first raced in 1887, the only opponent it faced was the clock.

Real racing did not appear until the 1890s, with the emergence of the petrol engine as a serious rival to steam. The first proper contest, run over a 128-km (80-mile) route from Paris to Rouen in 1894, was more of a trial than a race; its aim was to find the car which best satisfied the requirements "of being free from danger, easily handled by the travellers, and not too costly on the road". The demand for a competition between horseless carriages was shown by the 102 hopefuls who entered, anxious to demonstrate the superiority of their systems of propulsion. Only 21

cars actually made the start of the event, which was followed by a reporter sent by James Gordon Bennett, the proprietor of the *New York Herald*.

If the Paris–Rouen event proved anything, it was the superiority of the petrol car, with all the steam cars finishing at the bottom of the list. When a proper race, from Paris to Bordeaux and back, was organized the following year, only petrol cars qualified. The winner, Emile Levassor, covered the 1,178-km (732-mile) course solo in 48 hours 48 minutes, sustained only by a cup of broth and a glass of champagne at the halfway stage.

America's first race followed later the same year. Organized by the *Chicago Times-Herald* newspaper, it attracted nearly 100 entries, but on race day only two cars turned up. The event was postponed for 26 days in the hope that more cars might be ready, and six eventually started. All six entries were American-built, although three were modified Benz cars. Despite slushy weather, a Duryea, driven by J. Frank Duryea, and a Benz, driven by Oscar Mueller, finished the 87-km (54-mile) race – the two cars which had appeared on the original race day. The Duryea was America's first production car.

▲ **STEAM POWER**

Here, a De Dion steam car competes in the 1894 Paris–Rouen race. The steam cars were no match for their petrol-driven rivals.

# THE DEVELOPMENT OF RACING

Racing moved on apace after these early contests. France became the leader in road-racing, and as early as 1897 the press was complaining that "the amateur on his genuine touring car of 3 hp or 4.5 hp [1.2 litres] stood very little chance against the manufacturer, who was able to turn out a special racing monster of 8 hp [2.0 litres]". By 1899 racing was becoming more formalized. The first 2,500 km (1,550-mile) Tour de France for cars was announced, and a code of flag signals began to be developed. Racing cars developed a different character from touring models, and progress was so rapid that cars could become outdated in a matter of months. Where racing cars had managed with engines of six or eight horsepower in 1898, by 1899 16 and 20 horsepower were the norm. Wheelbases were made longer and the centre of gravity was lowered to make the cars more stable, while wheels – which on early cars had been smaller at the front, following the design of horse-carriages – were made the same size.

In 1901 the German Daimler company astounded the world with its new Mercedes car, which combined all the latest advances for the first time – pressed-steel chassis frame, honeycomb radiator, H-gate gear change, and mechanically operated inlet valves. It dominated racing at the Nice meeting in March that year and its design became the accepted pattern for fast cars. These features which had given it supremacy were quickly adapted for production cars.

▲ CITY TO CITY

An 18-hp De Dion Bouton followed by a 70-hp Mors are pictured here during the 1903 Paris–Madrid road race. Mors cars dominated these city-to-city races, which tested vehicle and driver to the limit.

The future pattern of racing was set by the Gordon Bennett series of races, inaugurated in 1900. These laid down detailed international rules governing the construction of racing cars and the organization of races. Significantly, in 1903 the race switched from being contested on a city-to-city basis to being run on a closed circuit. The cars built for the Gordon Bennett series represented the high point of an era when the simplest way to get more power was to

▶ MERCEDES WINNER

This is a 60-hp Mercedes of the type driven to victory in the 1903 Gordon Bennett by Camille Jenatzy.

build a bigger engine. For example, the 1905 Star had a capacity of 10.2 litres and was capable of 160 kph (100 mph). Such cars demanded enormous concentration and strength from the drivers who raced them over unsurfaced, dusty roads for hours on end.

The terms of the Gordon Bennett restricted each country taking part to just three entries. When the French won the trophy outright in 1905, they declared that they would institute a new race – the Grand Prix – which would give every company building racing cars an equal chance of winning. Since France had the world's premier motor car industry, it was assumed that the event would be a walkover for their national makers. Ironically, the plan backfired; although a French Renault won the first Grand Prix in 1906, the race went to Italy in 1907 and Germany in 1908. The French industry then voted to withdraw from racing on the pretext that "building and tuning special machines of this type meant a large expenditure of time and money, and the makers very naturally disliked the disorganization of their routine which resulted".

However, the makers very quickly found that their ban on racing resulted in lessened public interest in motor cars. By 1912 they were forced to revive the

▲ **HUNGARIAN RHAPSODY**

This ceramic tile panel shows the Hungarian driver Ferenc Szisz driving the winning Renault in the 1906 Grand Prix.

Grand Prix series. Although the engines of some of the competing cars were still large, the Grand Prix was run in conjunction with the Coupe de l'Auto event, which had a capacity limit of three litres. And while the first three cars home were still monsters – a 7.6-litre Peugeot and two 14.1-litre Fiats – they were closely followed by three 3-litre Sunbeams. Size still mattered to some extent, but it was becoming less important, because the twin overhead camshaft design of the winning Peugeot had unlocked the route to increased engine efficiency.

The rapid changes in formula meant that cars were quickly outmoded on the Grand Prix scene. However, outdated European cars could still gain success in America. In 1913 Frenchman Jules Goux won the Indianapolis 500 in his 1912 Grand Prix Peugeot, sustained by a bottle of champagne shared with his mechanic at each of his six pit stops. The following year his compatriot René Thomas came first in a 1913 Grand Prix Delage, followed by a Peugeot, another Delage, and a second Peugeot. The first American finisher, Barney Oldfield, in a Stutz, could manage no better than fifth. Though racing continued at Indianapolis while Europe was at war, only ceasing in 1917 and 1918, there was no American winner until 1920, when Gaston Chevrolet drove a four-

▼ **ONE-SEAT WONDER**

Ray Harroun won the first Indianapolis 500 in 1911 in this 7.8-litre six-cylinder Marmon Wasp, the world's first single-seater racing car.

**▲ SUCCESSFUL EXPORT**

The 1913 6.2-litre Grand Prix Delage, seen here racing at Le Mans, was one of several European cars that were successful in America in the early decades of the twentieth century.

cylinder 3-litre twin-cam Monroe to victory. One area where America was ahead of Europe, however, was sponsorship, with cars and drivers being sponsored by businesses from the 1920s onwards.

## THE TWENTIES

By the 1920s, racing had taken on distinctly national characteristics. France, which held the premier race, still known simply as the "Grand Prix", believed in racing on long road circuits. In Britain, where any kind of speed event on public roads was banned by law, racing centred on Brooklands, the world's first purpose-built race circuit. In America, apart from the Indianapolis circuit, built in 1911, there were mile and half-mile oval dirt tracks in most sizeable towns and on every county fairground. Laid down for horse-racing, these tracks were even more exciting when cars were run on them. There were also the board tracks, which provided the fastest racing in the world, but only had a short active life due to the effect of wear and weather.

Rising to the challenge of the top European marques, America struck back in the early 1920s with the nation's first victory in a major European race, when Jimmy Murphy's overhead cam straight-

eight Duesenberg won the 1921 French Grand Prix. Like Duesenberg's recently launched luxury road cars, the Grand Prix racer had the advanced feature of four-wheel hydraulic brakes. Fitted with a Miller engine, Murphy's Duesenberg went on to win the 1922 Indianapolis 500.

Duesenberg had a technical edge over other American makers, having built a wartime 16-valve aeroengine. Consequently, dirt track racing was dominated by Duesenberg-engined cars. Racing led Duesenberg to develop the thin-wall bearing because the old cast-babbitt bearings were melting at racing speeds. Top Duesenberg drivers were Tommy Milton, who won the 1919 Elgin Road Race, Jimmy Murphy, Ralph de Palma, and Pete dePaolo, who was the first driver to beat the 160 kph (100 mph) average at Indianapolis and won the national championship in 1925.

The 1920s were a period of technological experiment. For instance, in 1923 aerodynamicist Edmund Rumpler, who had designed Germany's much-feared Taube monoplane, created a Grand Prix car for Benz that was decades ahead of its time, with a teardrop-shaped body, swing-axle rear suspension, four-wheel brakes (inboard at the rear), and a mid-mounted twin-cam 2-litre engine. This "Tropfenwagen" may have been a technological marvel, but it only competed in one race, the Grand Prix de l'Europe at Monza, in which the two Benz entries finished fourth and fifth.

France's leading wartime aircraft builder, Gabriel Voisin, constructed an amazing "laboratory on wheels" for the 1923 Tours Grand Prix. It had racing's first aerodynamic monocoque body and was powered by a 2-litre six-cylinder sleeve-valve engine similar to that used on Voisin's road cars. The "Laboratoire" managed to finish a creditable fifth against far more powerful opposition. However, it had little effect on the general trend of racing car design. Another revolutionary racer which failed to make the impression it deserved was the 1925 Alvis sprint car that made its debut at the Kop Hillclimb in Buckinghamshire, in March 1925. Not only was it the world's first racer with a De Dion-type front axle for improved handling, but it also had a semi-monocoque Duralumin chassis.

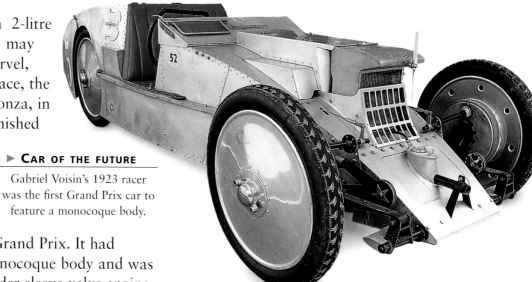

► **CAR OF THE FUTURE**
Gabriel Voisin's 1923 racer was the first Grand Prix car to feature a monocoque body.

Like many competition cars of its day, the Alvis sprint car was supercharged.

Experiments with forced induction went back to 1907, when Lee Sherman Chadwick of Pottstown, Pennsylvania, fitted a belt-driven supercharger to the racing version of his Great Chadwick Six luxury car. Mercedes, who had supercharged their World War I aeroengines in an attempt to increase performance at high altitudes, produced supercharged sports cars from the early 1920s. However, it was Fiat who first fitted a supercharger to a Grand Prix car. Experiments began in 1922, and the new straight-eight 2-litre Grand Prix car built for the 1923 season initially appeared with a vane-type blower driven from the nose of the crankshaft. But in their first race, the cars retired with supercharger trouble, and a hasty

▲ **DESIRABLE COMMODITY**
This 1921 advertising poster for the 10/32-hp Szawe shows how motor racing was used to promote production cars.

redesign saw the replacement of the faulty units with Roots-type superchargers. Reliability and power increased dramatically, and a supercharged Fiat won the Grand Prix of Europe at Monza in September 1923, giving Fiat the satisfaction of having won the first-ever victory for a supercharged Grand Prix car on home ground.

The most remarkable of the supercharged Grand Prix cars of the 1920s was the twin overhead camshaft straight-eight Delage. This first appeared for the opening season of the 1.5-litre formula in 1926, but an ill-conceived exhaust run burned the drivers' feet. Completely redesigned for 1927, with the exhaust moved to the nearside and one large supercharger instead of the twin blowers used the year before, the Delages won every major event on the motor-racing calendar – and they were still winning frontline races a decade later.

It was another French maker, Ettore Bugatti, who produced the most famous racing car of the decade, the Type 35, which made its debut at the 1924 Lyons Grand Prix. It revolutionized pitstop practice with its brilliant cast-aluminium wheels, which had integral brake drums so that the brake linings could be inspected and, if necessary, changed along with the tyres while the car was in the pits. The Type 35 was among the first Grand Prix cars that could be bought over the counter and raced "straight from the box". It was produced in both supercharged and naturally aspirated

▲ **CONSISTENT WINNERS**

Miller racers dominated the race photographed here. Harry Miller's designs were almost unbeatable in the board track races that were the staple of American motorsport between the wars.

formats in capacities of up to 2.3 litres and won literally hundreds of events in the 1920s. Possessed of a fearsome acceleration, the race-bred Type 35 Bugatti had a channel section chassis that varied in depth according to the stresses likely to be imposed on it. The T35's body seen from above was a symmetrical aerofoil section, and it remains one of the most beautiful racing cars ever produced.

America had a rival to Bugatti in Harry Miller, another artist-engineer who had no formal training, and who claimed that his brilliant designs came to him in a vision. "Somebody is telling me what to do," he professed. Miller became America's leading maker of racing engines between the wars. Aided by draughtsman Leon Goossen and machinist Fred Offenhauser, he built meticulously crafted twin-cam racers which swept the board in race after race and won a string of victories at Indianapolis. His glory days culminated in the early 1930s with V16 racers and a pair of four-wheel-drive cars, but though Miller's pursuit of perfection led him into bankruptcy in 1933, his designs lived on in the immortal Offenhauser, or "Offy", engine, the mainstay of American racing for decades.

◄ **WORK OF GENIUS**

This supercharged 1.5-litre straight-eight Miller 91 was designed in 1926. With a top speed of 280 kph (170 mph), it was a difficult car to beat.

## GERMAN SUPREMACY

In 1934 the Grand Prix rules changed once again to a maximum weight formula. Germany's newly elected chancellor Adolf Hitler used the new formula as a means of promoting the international image of German engineering. He offered an annual premium of half-a-million Reichsmarks (£41,600) to firms producing successful racing cars. Mercedes and Auto Union needed little prompting to accept the bait, with the result that German cars dominated motor racing right up to the outbreak of World War II.

Significantly, the German motor-racing programme produced the first successful rear-engined Grand Prix racer, Ferdinand Porsche's Auto Union P-Wagen, powered by a mid-mounted 4.4-litre V16 engine driving the rear wheels through a five-speed gearbox. It made its debut by setting new speed records on the banked AVUS track in Berlin, then won two Grands Prix in its first season, three in its second, and enjoyed sensational success in 1936 and 1937. Auto Union claimed that the 2.5 million Reichsmarks (£208,000) they spent on motor racing annually – the equivalent of one per cent of the company's turnover – had

▲ **POWER DISPLAY**

The Nürburgring circuit was the showcase for the mighty German racers of the 1930s such as the Mercedes W125 "Silver Arrows" and the Auto Union P-Wagen, designed by Porsche.

established the name of Auto Union as an important manufacturer of quality cars. A British government report published that "the prestige of German engineering was heightened wherever the superlative performance of these machines was witnessed".

The return of peace after World War II unleashed the pent-up demand for motor racing. Although most European circuits were either temporarily or permanently out of action due to the war – often from having been used as military storage areas – the determination of the enthusiasts to see motor racing revived surmounted that obstacle by finding new venues. Only four months after VE-Day, Europe held its first postwar motor race, in which a ragbag of prewar sports

▲ **SILVER DREAM RACER**

This 1937 5.7-litre Mercedes W125 was a successful product of the state-sponsored German racing programme.

and racing cars competed on a circuit created on the internal roads of Paris's Bois de Boulogne. Grand Prix racing followed two years later.

There were no new racing cars in the immediate postwar days, but there was a new international controlling body. In 1946 the French revised the old AIACR – the Association Internationale des Automobiles Clubs Reconnus – which had drawn up the prewar rules of racing, to create the Federation Internationale de l'Automobile, which in turn created Formula One as the premier racing class.

## THE POSTWAR ERA

America had largely gone its own way during the depressed 1930s, struggling to lure manufacturers back into motor racing with a "stock-block" formula that was a world away from the big budget, big horsepower activities of the Germans. This low-budget formula enabled would-be racers to buy a car capable of withstanding not only the Indianapolis Motor Speedway but also a season on the country dirt tracks with minimal maintenance. Manufacturers lured back by stock-block racing included Studebaker, who in 1932 built five racers based on the production 5.5-litre President straight-eight. Chrysler, Hudson, and Ford also raced: Ford with front-wheel-drive V8s built by Harry Miller in 1935. From 1939 to 1941 American racing was dominated by Offy-powered dirt-track cars, but the most successful Indianapolis 500 racer was Wilbur Shaw's "Boyle Special" Maserati which won the Indianapolis, or "Indy" 500 in 1939 and 1940.

After World War II, America's racing stock was quite different from that available in Europe. It featured a large number of very similar chassis and engines, so that races were much more closely contested. When Europe went over to the new 1.5 litres supercharged/4.5 litres unsupercharged formula in 1950, America stuck with the old 3.0 litres supercharged/4.5 litres unsupercharged rules. However, the prewar weight limitation was dropped to encourage light cars developed for dirt-track racing to compete at Indianapolis.

While keeping the old rules, America brought its "can do" attitude of mind to motor racing. A host of technological innovations were introduced by

American engineers. Many of these came from their experience in the nation's aviation industry. Offenhauser, for instance, made over $200,000-(£50,000-) worth of precision components a year for the Lockheed Lightning fighter and Constellation transport during the war. From aircraft design, racing took such things as tubular spaceframe construction, turbochargers, disc brakes, and fuel injection. High-octane Avgas fuel gave the edge to a highly successful American racer of the immediate postwar period, Lou Moore's "Blue Crown Special", which had front-wheel drive to cut frontal area and keep the centre of gravity low. Avgas gave three-times the fuel economy of the alcohol-based fuel used by rival marques, enabling the Blue Crown to go 500 miles with only one pit stop.

American designers had settled on the inline four as the optimum configuration for a racing car engine, but there was no such consensus in Europe. Ferrari began racing with Giaocchino Colombo's V12 engine, then moved to four cylinders when there were so few Formula One cars available that Grands Prix had to be run to Formula Two regulations. Alfa Romeo re-entered racing with an updated version of the prewar Tipo 158 straight-eight Alfetta, which was also designed by Colombo.

### ▲ ALFA'S RETURN

The 158 straight-eight Alfetta, seen here at Monza in 1948, was the basis for Italian manufacturer Alfa Romeo's return to motor racing after World War II.

The 1950s in America saw radical changes. Frank Kurtis built a turbocharged Diesel Indy racer for Cummins in 1952 – the first turbo car to run at Indianapolis – and laid the tall engine on its side to bring its height down. He used a tubular spaceframe with a close-fitting aluminium skin and sat the driver down low alongside the offset driveshaft. This "track roadster" set the pattern for Indy racers until the 1960s. But the Offy continued to be the pre-eminent engine, powering almost every American racer right through the 1950s and into the 1960s.

In Britain, it was the little Connaught and Vanwall marques that made the best showing in Grand Prix racing in the 1950s, with Connaught winning the country's first Grand Prix victory since the 1920s at Syracuse in the US in 1955. Vanwall established Britain as a serious Grand Prix contender. Their ingenious twin-cam engine had a Rolls-Royce-designed bottom end and a cylinder head based on that of the racing Norton motorbike, complete with hairpin valve springs. However, the eagerly awaited and much vaunted 1.5-litre V-16 BRM, with two-stage supercharging, proved a disappointment, its only successes being in minor races.

The 1948 launch of the Jaguar XK120, with its tireless six-cylinder twin-cam engine, heralded the opening of a glorious era for Britain in endurance racing. National fortunes had been in the doldrums since Bentleys had won five of the first eight Le Mans 24-hour races in the 1920s. A dedicated competition version of the XK120, the new tubular-framed

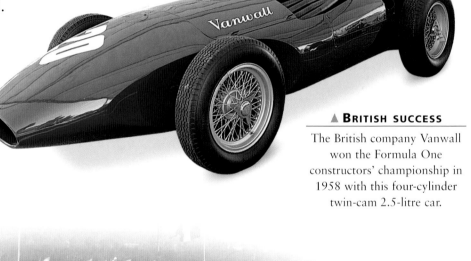

### ▲ BRITISH SUCCESS

The British company Vanwall won the Formula One constructors' championship in 1958 with this four-cylinder twin-cam 2.5-litre car.

### ▼ ENTER THE JAGUAR

The 1953 Le Mans 24-hour race was a triumph for Jaguar whose C-Types finished in first and second place.

C-Type (or XK120C) appeared in 1951 and won a first-time-out victory at Le Mans, thanks in part to its improved Lockheed drum front brakes.

At the 1952 Easter Goodwood meeting, Stirling Moss drove the 1951 Le Mans winner, XKC003, now fitted with aircraft-pattern disc brakes. That June, Moss achieved the first victory for a disc-braked car, driving its sister car XKC005 in the 358-km (224-mile) Reims Sports Car Grand Prix. Disc-braked C-Types were first and second at Le Mans in 1953. The aerodynamic monocoque D-Type followed, notching up three successive victories at Le Mans, crowned with a stunning first, second, third, fourth, and sixth place in 1957.

Germany did not feature in international motor racing for several years after World War II, but in 1952 Mercedes unveiled their 300SL competition coupé, with the distinctive "gullwing" doors that were a neat solution to the problem of access imposed by the car's light yet strong lattice-girder tubular chassis. Again, it was wartime aeroengine experience that led to the adoption of fuel injection, tested during the fallow 1953 season and producing a 14-bhp increase in power output compared with the carburetted version. Fuel injection was adopted as standard equipment for 1954 and was used in the desmodromic-valve 300SLR sports racer and the W196 which marked the return of the Silver Arrows to Grand Prix racing. In its initial form, the W196 featured full-width streamlined bodywork, but this made its handling erratic, and the cars were converted to open-wheel configuration.

The established front-engine layout for racing cars in the 1950s followed a pattern that could be traced back to the racing Panhard-Levassors of the 1890s. Remarkably, change was seeded in the London suburb of Surbiton, Surrey, where the Cooper company built 500cc racers powered by motorcycle engines. These dominated Formula Three racing in the late 1940s and early 1950s. The engines were positioned behind the driver and drove the rear axle via a chain. Cooper also built front-engined sports and racing cars, but they employed their proven rear-engined layout for their Coventry-Climax-engined sports car in 1955; and a single-seat derivative gave Australian Jack Brabham his entrée into Grand Prix racing.

▲ **BRILLIANT DEBUT**

Driver Karl Kling and his mechanic make running repairs to the winning 3-litre six-cylinder Mercedes 300SL during the Carrera Panamericana road race in 1952.

The 1958 Grand Prix season opened with a shock for the front-engined establishment when Stirling Moss's rear-engined Cooper-Climax beat the Ferraris of Musso and Hawthorn in the Argentine Grand Prix. Before long, the rear-engined route was the only one to follow for Grand Prix victory. Colin Chapman kept the front-engined configuration for his Lotus single-seaters, which were as economical in frontal area as the Coopers but were unreliable.

## THE REAR-ENGINED REVOLUTION

Chapman soon became an enthusiastic convert to the rear-engine configuration. Ever since the first Austin Seven-based Lotus "Trials Special", which had a stressed-skin marine-ply body and split front-axle beam the Lotus name had been synonymous with innovation and the razor-sharp mind of the company's founder. Trained as an aeronautical engineer, Chapman also drew on the aerodynamic skills of designer Frank Costin. The 1962 Lotus 25 was the first successful Grand Prix car to have a stressed-skin hull – it contained extra fuel tankage for the thirsty Coventry Climax V8 engine – and it featured a laid-back driving position which cut the frontal area of the car to a mere 0.75 sq m (8 sq ft).

Like most things in rear-engined racing, the first shot in the rear-engined campaign at Indianapolis was fired by Cooper. The old Brickyard had seen rear engines before, most notably on the prewar Gulf-Millers, but the disappointing performance of

these four-wheel drive bolides had not encouraged others to follow the same course. Jack Brabham raced a 2.7-litre Cooper-Climax at Indianapolis in 1961 and finished ninth in a field of 33 cars which all had engines of 4.2 litres. California hot-rodder Mickey Thompson saw that this vision of the future worked as well on the oval at Indianapolis as it had on the twisting circuits of Europe, and built an all-American rear-engined car with Buick V8 power for the 1962 Indianapolis 500.

Englishman Colin Chapman went to Indianapolis in 1962 and met a group of executives from Ford's Dearborn headquarters. Chapman left with a contract to build three rear-engined cars for the 1963 Indy 500. The resulting Lotus 29 – a long-wheelbase development of the Type 25 Grand Prix racer fitted with a 4.2-litre push-rod "stock-block" Ford V8 engine – was driven at Indianapolis by Jim Clark. Clark should, in the eyes of many, have won, because the winner, American Parnelli Jones, was dropping oil on the track from his Watson and should have been called into the pits.

There was no mistake in 1965, however, when Clark's Len Terry-designed Lotus 38, which had a monocoque body and offset fuel-injected quad-cam 4.2-litre Ford V8 power unit, romped home to the first-ever over 240-kph (150-mph) victory. The day

### ▲ FIRST ATTEMPT

This Lotus 29 was Colin Chapman's first attempt at developing a car to win the Indy 500. Based on the Lotus 25 Grand Prix car, the Lotus 29 came second at Indianapolis in 1963.

of the front-engined racer at Indianapolis was over and 1966 saw another British win, when Graham Hill drove his Ford-powered "American Red Ball Special" (in actual fact a Lola from Slough, Berkshire) into Victory Lane.

The Lola GT sports racer was the inspiration for one of the most successful endurance racers of the 1960s, the Ford GT40, whose origins lay in an abortive attempt by Ford to buy Ferrari in 1963. The deal had been called off at the eleventh hour by Enzo Ferrari, who was alarmed by the nitpicking investigations of the Ford accountants. Ford set up the Ford Advanced Vehicles division in Slough to develop a sports racer capable of winning Le Mans and wresting the initiative from Ferrari.

The 4.7-litre GT40 (so-called because it stood just 40 inches high) proved to be the fastest racing coupé in the world, and won a spectacular 1-2-3

### ◄ AMERICAN DREAM

This programme for Le Mans depicts one of the stylish endurance racers of the 1960s. The 1966 Le Mans was dominated by Ford whose Mark II GT40 shown below, came first, second, and third.

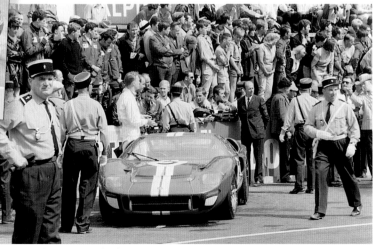

victory in the 1966 Le Mans, when three Mk IIs crossed the finishing line abreast. In 1967, Ford won a second Le Mans with the new Mk IV GT, which had a bonded aluminium honeycomb hull and 500-bhp 7-litre engine. Ford's racing programme was continued in 1968 and 1969 by JW Automotive, whose 4.7-litre GT40 No. 1075 won at Le Mans in both years.

## MODERN TECHNOLOGY

The 1960s also saw Ford play a crucial role in Formula One racing after the sport's principal engine supplier, Coventry Climax, decided that the cost of developing a new engine to meet the new 3-litre regulations was prohibitive. In 1965 Colin Chapman used his contacts with Ford of Britain to persuade the corporation to finance the £100,000 development costs of a new Cosworth V8 Grand Prix engine. The new engine would be exclusive to Lotus for its first season, and available to other teams thereafter. The DFV – "Double Four Valve" – Grand Prix engine was installed in the new Lotus 49 Formula One car, which won its first race, the 1967 Dutch Grand Prix, driven by Jim Clark. That victory was the first of an all-time record of 155 Formula One wins for the Ford engine.

Chapman had another first when he unveiled the 1968 Lotus 49B, a modified version of the 49, which Graham Hill drove to victory in that year's world championship. Instead of the traditional Lotus green livery it ran in Gold Leaf Team Lotus colours. Sponsorship paint schemes had been a feature of racing at Indianapolis since the 1920s, but they came as something of a shock when they displaced national colours on the more conservative European scene.

The late 1960s saw a brief flirtation with four-wheel drive among the Formula One

### ▶ JET-SETTER

This four-wheel-drive Lotus 56B is the only Grand Prix car to have been powered by a gas turbine. It was raced in 1971 by Emerson Fittipaldi.

constructors, and the introduction of ludicrously high-mounted wings as chassis engineers used aerodynamic know-how to improve cornering power. These wings were banned, but more rational wings appeared as extensions of the bodywork. In parallel, bodies became more wedge-shaped until, in 1977, arch rule-bender Colin Chapman brought out his "ground-effect" Lotus 78. This car had sidepods shaped like inverted aerofoils and was fitted with sliding skirts to close the gap between car and ground so that the racer's passage through the air sucked the car down on to the track for greater cornering power. The Type 78 gave Lotus the world championship for 1979, because Chapman's rivals failed to learn from his pioneering tactics. However, by the end of 1980 ground-effect had been banned.

With ground-effect a thing of the past, a new Grand Prix scenario dawned in 1983, with turbo-chargers a near essential. Like supercharging, turbocharging technology originated with the aircraft industry. Instead of being positively driven by gears, chains, or belts like a supercharger, a turbocharger uses the gases in the exhaust pipe to drive a turbine wheel which, in turn, spins a rotary-vane compressor to pump air into the combustion chamber. The molecules in compressed air become heated and try to expand, and to counter this an

"intercooler" is placed between the turbocharger and cylinder to cool the fuel/air mix. A wastegate or "blow-off" valve acts as a safety valve, releasing excess pressure. In the 1980s, Renault Grand Prix engineers discovered that injecting water into the incoming charge stimulated combustion and increased power; Renault even dispensed with the wastegate. Ultimately, turbocharged Grand Prix engines, operating at five times atmospheric pressure, were producing up to 1100 hp. A restriction to four-times atmospheric pressure in 1987 did little to halt the surge in horsepower, and cars such as the McLaren-Honda MP4/4 were running on the edge of self-destruction. This potentially lethal situation was addressed when new regulations in 1988 brought an end to the era of the 1000-bhp Grand Prix engine.

Compared with Formula One, the rules of the Indianapolis 500 remained fairly consistent, and ground-effect was still permitted after moveable skirts were banned. Ground force equivalent to three-times the weight of the car could be produced, sufficient to hold the cars to the track at speeds of up to 360 kph (225 mph). Most of the successful Indy cars and engines were built in Britain, with the turbocharged Cosworth DFX (a short-stroke 2.65-litre development of the DFV) providing power for ten Indianapolis winners during the 1960s and 1970s. Chassis were supplied by March and Lola; and

▲ **CHEQUERED FLAG**

Alain Prost takes the chequered flag in the turbocharged McLaren-Honda MP4/4 at the 1988 Australian Grand Prix at Adelaide.

even Penske, despite their all-American image, had their cars built at a factory in Dorset.

Lotus showed in 1987 that the team's inventiveness had not died in 1982 with company founder Colin Chapman. The new Lotus 99T, with its single-sheet carbon/Kevlar monocoque, offered "active" suspension that maintained optimum ride height as the fuel load varied throughout a Grand Prix. The introduction of new compound materials brought tremendous changes to chassis design, as they were light but immensely strong. As early as the mid-1960s Ford were using an aluminium honeycomb material to make the chassis tubs of their GT "J-Cars" for Le Mans; and aluminium honeycombs continue to play a very important role in racing car chassis construction, but are now sandwiched between layers of carbon-composite materials to make a strong laminate.

► **WINNING COMBINATION**

The 1997 McLaren-Mercedes, driven here by David Coulthard at Silverstone, combines the expertise of two of the great names in motor sport.

The various panels of carbon-composite which go to make up the chassis are built up and bonded with resin in moulds taken from a highly accurate full-scale model of the finished unit. The aluminium honeycomb varies in thickness, according to the stresses imposed on it in service, and incorporates aluminium or Tufnol resin mounting-points for bolts and other structural fittings. A typical Formula One chassis weighs only 35 kg (80 lb), yet can handle some 750 hp and withstand a demanding series of crash tests without failure. Indeed, one test ensures that the cockpit sides would not collapse if they were hit by an airborne car in a multiple crash.

Aerodynamics are a major factor in maintaining the performance of racing cars in the face of the efforts of the regulators to curb speed on the track. Although new rules for 1998 were intended to cut downforce by 15 per cent, the aerodynamicists were well on the way to overcoming the handicap by fine-tuning their designs over the course of the season. Designers have been aware, for nearly a hundred years, of the effect that airflow over a car plays in its performance; but it is only since the late 1960s that it has come to be the most important factor in racing car design. At least one leading racing car designer now claims that 80 per cent of his car's performance depends on aerodynamic efficiency, which governs cornering power as well as straight-line speed. A major problem in automobile aerodynamics has been the fact that, unlike an aircraft, a car does not move cleanly through the air, but remains on the road, which alters the characteristics of the airflow beneath the vehicle. This has been the main penalty that the ground-effect cars have attempted to overcome. Another problem is caused by the rotating mass of exposed wheels which create unavoidable aerodynamic

**▲ GLITTERING PRIZE**

This is the start of the 1995 Indianapolis 500, which was won by Jacques Villeneuve. The race is run every Memorial Day weekend for the Borg Warner Trophy and a million-dollar-plus prize.

drag. So all racing-car aerodynamicists concentrate on three factors – drag, downforce, and balance. These are fine-tuned during thousands of hours of wind-tunnel testing to make the machines fast yet stable.

As the millennium draws to a close, the motor-racing scene has a devoted following all round the world at all levels. More than a hundred years after people first discovered the excitement of racing, it still holds a fascination. The sight of a skilled driver controlling speed on the track is one that we all thrill to, whether it is a vintage Type 35 Bugatti storming round a circuit in the rain or a Grand Prix ace slipping though an almost impossible gap to gain the lead in a battle for the world championship. It may be debatable whether motor racing really does still improve the road-going breed, but it has produced some remarkable thoroughbreds of the track. Long may it continue!

# ULTIMATE
# RACING CARS

# 2

At each stage of automotive development, racing cars have come to represent the ultimate achievement in power, speed, and technology, and car design has constantly pushed the boundaries of driving and engineering skills. A car that could reach 50 kph (30 mph) in the Victorian days was every bit as exciting to drive as a modern racer capable of exceeding 350 kph (200 mph); to the true acifionado both cars are equally as interesting. Nowadays, we are fortunate that we can witness the best of the old and the best of the new in action, thanks to the unending dedication and enthusiasm that inspires motor racing at all levels. Each season brings new, unanticipated challenges for racing-car designers and drivers, and every season brings new excitements for the millions of enthusiasts across the world who follow motor racing. This chapter presents the different cars – and circuits – that have made motor racing a sport unlike any other.

# 1900-1920

# THE EARLY YEARS

THE SECOND DECADE of the century saw the disappearance of the gigantic racers which had characterized the first phase of international racing. Engineers had gained a better understanding of how to get more power out of an engine by improving the design of cylinder heads and inlet and exhaust manifolds. The valve gear also became the subject of rapid development: overhead valves became more common on racing cars, and overhead camshafts became the preferred method of operating them. There was a growing appreciation of the effects of aerodynamics as well, for the aviation age had just dawned, and adventurous car builders began experimenting with streamlined bodywork. Sometimes, however, their experiments showed a certain lack of familiarity with even the most basic principles involved. The appearance of purpose-built tracks like Brooklands and Indianapolis also affected the design of racing cars, and the bold decision taken in 1911 by Marmon to drive solo without the riding mechanic in the passenger seat led to the creation of monoposto bodywork. This innovation, however, had little influence on the general trend of design.

◀ **HEROIC AGE**

Leather helmet, goggles, and a powerful racer – an enduring image depicting the heroic age of motor racing.

▼ **TWIN-CAM PIONEER**

The twin-cam racer pioneered by Peugeot revolutionized engine design on both sides of the Atlantic.

# 1900-1920 The Gordon Bennett Races

GORDON
BENNETT

THE FIRST international race series was the brainchild of an eccentric American newspaper proprietor, James Gordon Bennett. The participating countries each entered a team of three cars, selected by the national automobile clubs. Every part of a competing car – even the tyres – had to be produced in the country that it represented. The first race was run in 1900 and was won by a French car. Initially the Gordon Bennett races were run as part of city-to-city events, but in 1903 the event was staged over a closed circuit in Ireland. This set a precedent for a new series of races – the Grands Prix – which replaced the Gordon Bennett series in 1905.

### ▶ DEATH RACE

The French four-cylinder 70-hp Mors Dauphine was the dominant car in the last great city-to-city race in 1903. Intended to run between Paris and Madrid, there were so many accidents that the race was halted at Bordeaux.

Tubular chassis

### ▲ UNSUCCESSFUL CONTENDER

The 110-hp Gobron-Brillié had a huge 13.5-litre four-cylinder opposed-piston engine in a light tubular frame. It was the first car to exceed 160 kph (100 mph), in 1904. However, in spite of this achievement, it failed to qualify for the 1904 Gordon Bennett Cup.

### ◀ DUST AND DANGER

This 1903 painting by Manuel Roble shows a Mors hard on the heels of a fleeing Mercedes. The picture gives a vivid impression of the drama and danger of the early races.

### ▲ MIGHTY SAMSON

The 15.1-litre racing six-cylinder Napier "Samson", with its aggressively pointed tubular radiator, was the fastest car in the world, being capable of 170 kph (105 mph). It was chosen for the 1905 British Gordon Bennett team, finishing eighth.

Spare tyres    Mechanic's seat

▲ **BORROWED WINNER**

This chain-driven 60-hp Mercedes is the same as the borrowed car driven to victory by Camille Jenatzy in the 1903 Gordon Bennett race. Mercedes' 90-hp cars intended to race in 1903 were destroyed in a fire.

▲ **TWO-TIMES WINNER**

Frenchman Léon Théry, driving a four-cylinder 80-hp Richard-Brasier, wins the 1904 Gordon Bennett race. The car was uprated to 100 hp for the 1905 race, the last of the series, and Théry won again.

▲ **SOLE SURVIVOR**

Léonce Girardot sits on the four-litre 24-hp Panhard-Levassor which won the 1901 Gordon Bennett race, though it was the only competitor to finish.

Clarkson radiator    Tool box

▶ **BRITISH VICTORY**

A 1902 four-cylinder Napier won the Gordon Bennett race of that year. The car was unusual in having live-axle transmission rather than the more familiar chain drive.

Flywheel shield

Wooden chassis frame with iron flitch-plates

## 1900-1920 The Vanderbilt Cup

PUBLICITY
POSTER, 1911

WILLIAM KISSEM Vanderbilt Jr – known to his friends as "Willie K" – was a wealthy American sportsman. His love of motor sport prompted him, in 1904, to offer a trophy that would encourage American manufacturers to go racing. Open to cars of all nations, but held in the United States, the Vanderbilt Cup races exceeded all expectations. They were among the most exciting contests of the early days, inspiring exciting new car design. The earliest races – held on Long Island between 1904 and 1910 – were the best, and the biggest success in these contests was the Locomobile.

### ▼ CONVINCING WIN

Originally built for the 1906 Vanderbilt Cup race, this massive 16-litre Locomobile was redesigned for the 1908 event and fitted with detachable wheel rims to make tyre changing easier. Driven by 23-year-old George Robertson, the Locomobile won the race in record time.

### ▲ WELL CAUGHT!

When the spare tyre broke loose on Arthur Duray's 17-litre 130-hp Lorraine-Dietrich during the 1906 Vanderbilt Cup, his riding mechanic saved it but nearly fell overboard himself. Duray managed to hold on to the mechanic with one hand and steer with the other.

### ▶ FIRST-LAP LEADER

Eighteen-year-old American driver Spencer Wishart drove this four-cylinder 9.25-litre 60-hp Mercedes in the 1909 Vanderbilt Cup. The car held the lead for one lap but was then hampered by a broken fuel line, though it still managed to complete the race.

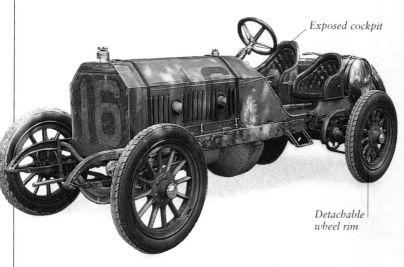

Exposed cockpit

Detachable wheel rim

Drive chain

### ◀ DOWN TO EARTH

The 1908 16-litre Locomobile is shown here being refuelled. The crew who looked after supplies of fuel, oil, and spares were located in a trench (the "pits"). In many early races, only the driver and his riding mechanic were allowed to work on the car during the event.

## ▲ PUNCTURED PRIDE

Joe Tracy sits at the wheel of the 16-litre Locomobile which was built especially for the 1906 Vanderbilt Cup. The Locomobile was the fastest car in the race, but its Achilles' heel proved to be the fixed-rim wheels which made tyre changing a laborious process.

## ▲ BAD CASE OF THE BENDS

Frank Croker tried to improve the power-to-weight ratio of his monstrous 75-hp Simplex by drilling holes in the chassis and axles. But he overstepped the limit, and the potholed course, with its humpbacked railway crossings, bent the chassis.

*Scarf to wipe goggles*

## ▲ HOME-GROWN WINNER

The winner of the 1911 Vanderbilt Cup was this all-American 8915cc 46-hp Lozier driven by Ralph Mulford. The Lozier beat off a good international entry that included Fiat, Mercedes, and Benz cars, and won at a record speed of 120 kph (74 mph).

## ▲ EUROPEAN CHALLENGE

William Luttgen awaits the start of the 1904 Vanderbilt Cup in his 60-hp Mercedes, powered by a 9.25-litre four-cylinder engine with overhead valves. Though it was Europe's finest racing car, the Mercedes finished two laps behind George Heath's winning Panhard.

*Beam axle*

# 1900-1920 Itala 120 hp

*OIL GAUGE*

FOUNDED IN 1904, Itala of Turin went racing from the start. Three 120-hp Italas were built, and although they were not ready to run in the 1907 French Grand Prix, the model here won that year's Coppa della Velocità at Brescia, Italy. In 1908, the British agent for Itala, H.R. Pope, took the car to Russia for the 692-km (430-mile) St Petersburg–Moscow race. It finished third, even though it broke both of its front springs crossing a humpbacked bridge. It was bought that year by a British enthusiast, Edgar Thornton, and was regularly driven on the road until his death in 1931.

▲ **WINNING CAR**

This Itala was driven to victory in the Coppa della Velocità in 1907 by Alessandro Cagno at an average speed of 104.9 kph (65.2 mph). Cagno was also the chauffeur to Queen Margherita of Italy.

▶ **THE MECHANICAL SIDE**

The Itala is powered by a massive four-cylinder engine with a capacity of 14.4 litres, designed to meet a fuel consumption formula of 30 litres/100 km (9.4 mpg). Unusually, at a time when most racers had chain drive, the Itala has a live axle geared to around 65 mph/1,000 rpm.

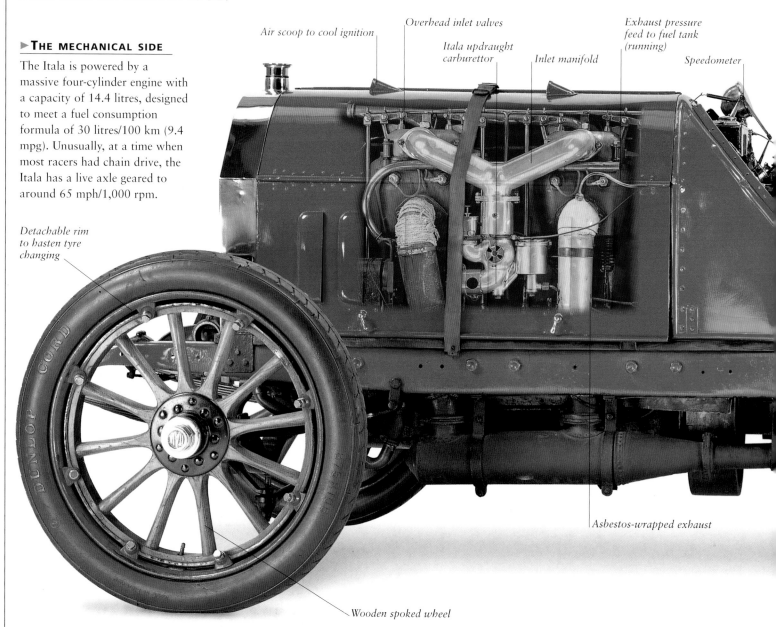

*Air scoop to cool ignition*

*Overhead inlet valves*

*Exhaust pressure feed to fuel tank (running)*

*Itala updraught carburettor*

*Inlet manifold*

*Speedometer*

*Detachable rim to hasten tyre changing*

*Asbestos-wrapped exhaust*

*Wooden spoked wheel*

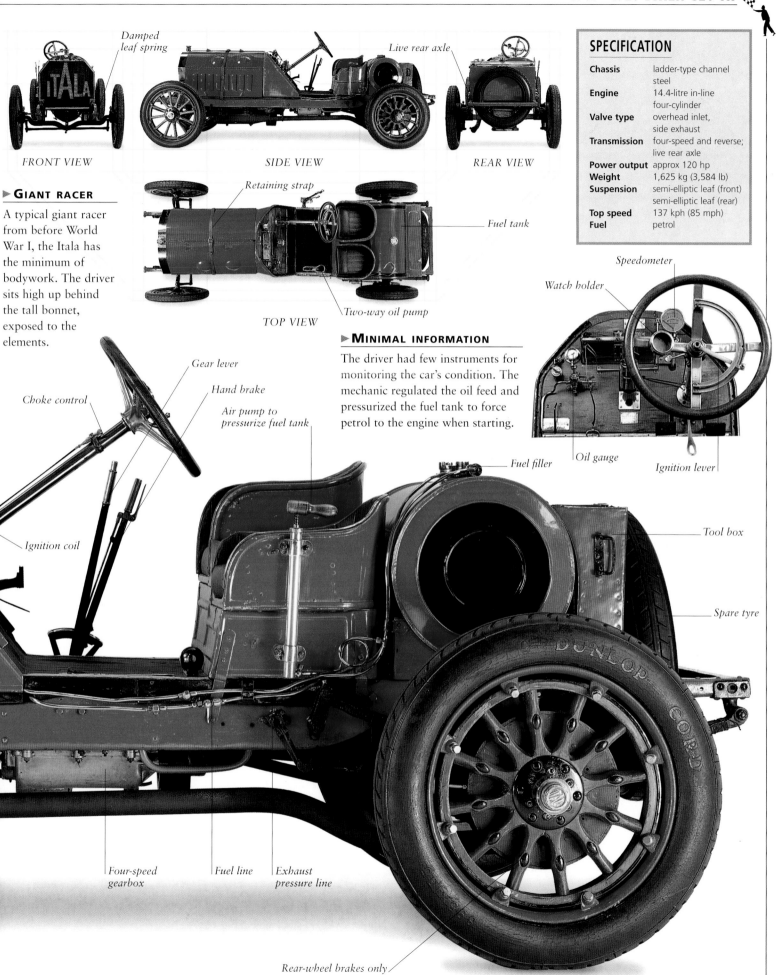

FRONT VIEW

SIDE VIEW

REAR VIEW

Damped
leaf spring

Live rear axle

## SPECIFICATION

| | |
|---|---|
| **Chassis** | ladder-type channel steel |
| **Engine** | 14.4-litre in-line four-cylinder |
| **Valve type** | overhead inlet, side exhaust |
| **Transmission** | four-speed and reverse; live rear axle |
| **Power output** | approx 120 hp |
| **Weight** | 1,625 kg (3,584 lb) |
| **Suspension** | semi-elliptic leaf (front) semi-elliptic leaf (rear) |
| **Top speed** | 137 kph (85 mph) |
| **Fuel** | petrol |

### ▶ GIANT RACER

A typical giant racer from before World War I, the Itala has the minimum of bodywork. The driver sits high up behind the tall bonnet, exposed to the elements.

Retaining strap

Fuel tank

TOP VIEW

Two-way oil pump

### ▶ MINIMAL INFORMATION

The driver had few instruments for monitoring the car's condition. The mechanic regulated the oil feed and pressurized the fuel tank to force petrol to the engine when starting.

Speedometer

Watch holder

Oil gauge

Ignition lever

Gear lever

Hand brake

Air pump to
pressurize fuel tank

Choke control

Ignition coil

Fuel filler

Tool box

Spare tyre

Four-speed
gearbox

Fuel line

Exhaust
pressure line

Rear-wheel brakes only

# 1900-1920 Racing around the World

*THE SPYKER IN THE PEKING–PARIS RACE*

THE EARLY YEARS of motor sports saw perhaps the most extraordinary races ever held – the Peking (Beijing)–Paris contest (1907) and the New York–Paris contest (1908). Race entries amounted to five or six cars each year. Run for the most part over trackless wastes, these round-the-world races were supreme endurance tests for both the drivers and the machines. They demonstrated how far car design and technology had progressed in only a few years, thanks to competition. The makers of the winning cars – an Itala and a Thomas-Flyer – were inundated with demands for new machines but failed to deliver a product that met with the originals' standards.

### ▶ HARD GOING

Montague Roberts drove the Thomas-Flyer on the first stage of the journey from New York to Paris. Poor road surfaces were a problem throughout the race. Roberts had to enlist the aid of local farmers to free his car from deep mud in Nebraska.

*Canvas scuttle cowl*

*Driving chain*

*Wooden spoked wheel*

### ▲ LATE ARRIVAL

The 24-hp 7.4-litre Züst reaches the finish of the 1908 New York–Paris race. Delayed by a crash in Germany just 500 miles short of the destination, it was nearly two months behind the first car to arrive.

### ◀ STUCK IN THE MUD

The little 10-hp De Dion-Bouton driven by Frenchman Victor Collignon had to be hauled out of deep mud on the Nankow road by horse power at the beginning of the 1907 Peking–Paris race.

### ▲ FIRST SIGHT OF A CAR

The Thomas-Flyer, driven by George Schuster, arrives at the Maibara Inn in rural Japan, where no car had ever been seen. New York–Paris contestants had hoped to drive across the Bering Straits, but they proved impassable, and the cars crossed the Pacific by boat.

*Oil sidelamp*

*Acetylene headlamp*

### ▲ MARATHON MOTORS

The 1907 Peking–Paris race was won by this 7.4-litre Itala 35/40 hp driven by Prince Scipione Borghese, a wealthy Italian sportsman. The car's three-man crew calculated that they had driven more than 8,000 miles (12,800 km) on their journey through Asia and Europe.

*Additional fuel tank*

*Spare tyre*

*Detachable mudguard for use as emergency bridge*

### ▲ WELL PRESERVED

This 60-hp 9.2-litre four-cylinder Thomas-Flyer looks today much as it did at the end of the New York–Paris race. Still carved on its front seat are the initials of spectators who cheered the first victory of an American car in international competition on its arrival in Paris in 1908.

### ◀ IN THE DEEP MIDWINTER

Bundled in furs against the snow, Züst driver Giulio Sartori prepares to leave Buffalo, New York, on his way west across the United States in the 1908 New York–Paris race. The car had no windshield, just a canvas cowling to protect its occupants from the freezing cold.

# 1900-1920 The Fiat Marque

FOUNDED IN 1899, Fiat – Fabbrica Italiana Automobili Torino – were a dominant force in the early days of motor racing. Huge racers, such as Mephistopheles, were built before World War I, then Fiat created the more sophisticated models of the 1920s. Fiat's twin-cam racers were so successful that Sunbeam replicated them in Britain; their version was known as the "Fiat in green paint". After the twin-cam cars, Fiat developed another winning formula, the supercharged Grand Prix cars. Although Fiat withdrew from Grands Prix in the late 1920s, the company continued to compete in events like the Mille Miglia with small sports cars. Today, Fiat are once again racing in Grands Prix through their subsidiary, Ferrari.

### ▲ NOT MEANT FOR MOUNTAINS

Fiat built this 7.4-litre four-cylinder racer with overhead valves for the first Targa Florio race in 1906. The race was run around the rough mountain roads of Sicily. Unfortunately, the car, driven by Fiat works driver Vincenzo Lancia, was not designed for such demanding road surfaces, and it had to be withdrawn.

### ▲ FIAT WINNER

In 1907 Felice Nazzaro's 7.8-litre Fiat won the Kaiserpreis, a race organized by Kaiser Wilhelm II. This contest was for "medium-powered touring cars" with engines of less than 8 litres. Nazarro was first in a field of 40 entrants.

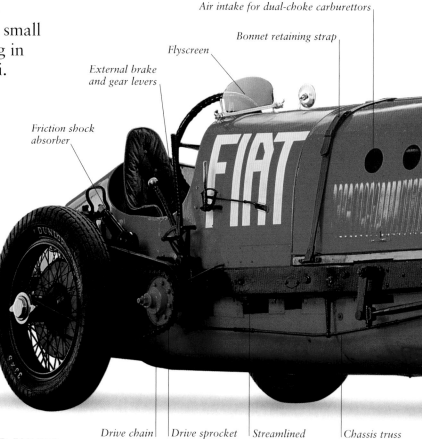

*Air intake for dual-choke carburettors*

*Bonnet retaining strap*

*Flyscreen*

*External brake and gear levers*

*Friction shock absorber*

*Drive chain*  *Drive sprocket*  *Streamlined undertray*  *Chassis truss bracing*

### ◄ OVERSIZED FAILURE

One of the cars built by Fiat for the 1914 French Grand Prix was this 4.5-litre model. It had twin overhead camshafts and four-wheel brakes. Its oversized engine would have led to disqualification, but the only one to finish came last.

### ▲ DEVIL OF A CAR

Mephistopheles was originally a 120-hp four-cylinder racer. Then in the early 1920s its owner Ernest Eldridge installed a huge 21.7-litre overhead-camshaft six-cylinder Fiat airship engine. To fit the new engine he had to lengthen the chassis by 45 cm (18 in).

## ▼ SUCCESSFUL SPORTS CAR

Fiat's 508S sports car, launched in 1933, was based on the Balilla 995cc family saloon. The boxy original was an unlikely basis for a racer, but with its SIATA overhead valve conversion this sporting version was a great success in the 1100cc sports car category for several years.

## ▲ DOUBLE SIZE

The Fiat Grand Prix car of 1907, in this tile panel, had a 15.3-litre engine, almost twice that of the Kaiserpreis racer. Felice Nazzaro drove it to victory in that year's Kaiserpreis and Targa Florio races.

*Specially fabricated radiator*

## ◄ DEVIL'S GALLOP

Ernest Eldridge raced Mephistopheles at Brooklands in the 1920s. The car could lap the circuit at over 175 kph (110 mph).

### RACING HIGHLIGHTS

**1900** Vincenzo Lancia and Felice Nazzaro driving early Fiat racers finish first and second in the Padua-to-Padua race.

**1907** Nazzaro wins the Grand Prix, Targa Florio, and Kaiserpreis races for Fiat.

**1908** Nazzaro wins Coppa Florio and, driving Mephistopheles, beats the Napier Samson in Brooklands match race.

**1911** Hemery wins the Grand Prix de France in a 10.5-litre S61 Fiat. David Bruce-Brown wins the Savannah Grand Prize in a 14.1-litre S74.

**1922** Nazzaro's twin-cam Fiat wins the French Grand Prix.

**1923** The Tipo 805 is the first successful supercharged Grand Prix car and wins the Italian Grand Prix.

**1924** Mephistopheles sets a new land speed record of 235 kph (146 mph).

*Lengthened chassis using sections of London bus frame*

*Brakeless front wheel*

## ► BIGGEST OF ALL

The biggest early Fiat racer was the "Beast of Turin", a 300-hp machine powered by a 28.3-litre airship engine. The car was reported to have been driven at 290 kph (180 mph) at Long Island, New York, in 1912. Its huge engine meant that the driver had to peer round the side of the bonnet to see where he was going.

# 1900-1920 France's Grandes Epreuves

*PEUGEOT ADVERTISING POSTER*

THE FRENCH GRAND Prix, which had replaced the Gordon Bennett series in 1906, was regarded as the world's premier motor race. However, it was suspended after France's crushing defeat by the German Mercedes and Benz cars in 1908 and not revived until 1912. In the interim there were other "grandes epreuves" – first class races which were not official Grands Prix. When the Grand Prix was reinstated, Peugeot brought victory back to France with their revolutionary twin-cam cars. Peugeot won again in 1913, but 1914 saw another German victory, with Mercedes cars in first, second, and third place.

### ◄ BIG IN AMERICA

The 4.5-litre L45 Peugeot was beaten by Mercedes in the 1914 French Grand Prix. However, the car carried on racing in the United States after war broke out in Europe. In 1915 it won the Vanderbilt Cup and the US Grand Prix. Dario Resta then drove it to victory in the 1916 Indianapolis 500.

*Compulsory two-man crew*

*High-level exhaust for horizontal-valve engine*

### ▲ OVERDRIVE GEAR

The French Type X Delage was fitted with the world's first five-speed overdrive transmission. The car was the runaway winner of the principal race of 1911, the Coupe de l'Auto for light cars of less than 3 litre-engine displacement.

*Knock-off Rudge-Whitworth wheels*

### ◄ STRONG CHALLENGE

Albert Guyot drove the Type Y four-cylinder Delage which was Peugeot's main challenger in the 1913 Grand Prix. The car's 6.2-litre engine developed 105 hp, and it had a four-speed gearbox. Guyot led for much of the race until the riding mechanic jumped out to change a tyre and was run over by his own car.

*Unbraked front wheels*

Bonnet retaining strap

Bolster fuel tank

## ▲ RACING MONSTER

This 14.1-litre Fiat competed in the revived Grand Prix of 1912. Although it looked positively Jurassic beside the modern, lighter designs from makers such as Peugeot and Rolland-Pilain, it still finished second.

## ▲ FAST FAVOURITE

The twin-cam 5.7-litre Peugeot, driven by Georges Boillot, started as favourite in the 1913 French Grand Prix. The race was run over 29 laps of a 31.6-km (19.5-mile) course near Amiens. Boillot's car, which touched over 156 kph (97 mph) on the straights, duly won.

Overflow pipe

Radiator stoneguard

## ▼ WINNING WAYS

The 1914 French Grand Prix was won by a four-cylinder Mercedes in a tense finish. The car's 4.5-litre engine could produce a top speed of 180 kph (112 mph). The driver, Christian Lautenschlager, harried the long-term leader, Peugeot driver Georges Boillot, until the strain forced him to retire.

## ▲ FOLLOWING THE TREND

Jean Chassagne drives this 3-litre twin-cam Sunbeam in the 1914 Grand Prix. Peugeot's successful twin-cam technology inspired its rivals to follow suit, and five of the 13 models in this race had twin overhead camshafts.

# 1920-1940

# THE GOLDEN AGE

FOR MANY, the racing cars built between the wars represent a golden age of motor sport. The 1920s saw the arrival of jewel-like racing cars such as Bugatti and Miller – hand-built marvels created by visionary artist-engineers. These cars enjoyed great success on the track, yet could be ordered from a catalogue – provided you were wealthy enough. Then came the straight-eight Delage, with its fearfully complex power unit. This model was still capable of winning races ten seasons after it had first been built. The glorious Jano-designed Alfa Romeos of the 1920s and 1930s were in a class of their own; they were wonderfully fluid to drive, yet with the staying power to dominate some of the toughest races ever run, such as Italy's fabulous Mille Miglia. There were also the mighty Silver Arrows of Germany, funded by a totalitarian state that wished to promote national pride through success in Grand Prix racing. The drivers who took to the steering wheel of these cars enjoyed the status of supermen, for their driving skills made them seem part of their car, like modern-day centaurs.

◄ **RETURN TO RACING**

The 500-Mile Race at Brooklands represented a return to "proper" racing, with fast cars of all sizes competing on a handicap basis.

▼ **NEW AT INDIANAPOLIS**

One of the most dramatic Indianapolis challengers was Harry Miller's 5-litre V16 racer which ran between 1931 and 1932.

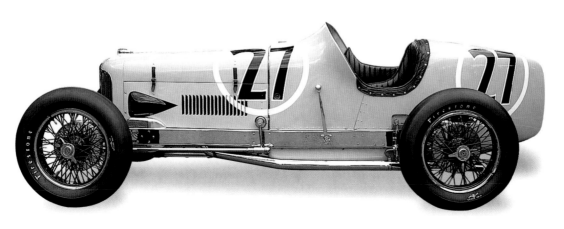

# 1920-1940 Racing at Brooklands

*1929 RACE PROGRAMME*

BY THE TIME Brooklands circuit closed in 1939, racing cars had reached speeds of over 240 kph (150 mph). The track was purpose-built in 1907 since road racing was illegal in England. Set in the grounds of landowner Hugh Locke-King's country home, Brooklands reached the height of its popularity in the 1920s, attracting huge crowds. With its 9.1-metre (30-foot) high cement bankings, the 4.4-km (2.75-mile) circuit was specifically designed for speeds exceeding 190 kph (120 mph).

## ▲ WHIRLWIND TECHNIQUE

Polish-born Count Stanislas Czaykowski drove this 4.9-litre straight-eight Bugatti T51 "like a whirlwind" to win the 1933 Empire Trophy Race at 198.84 kph (123.58 mph). The Bugatti T51 had been designed, built, and put on the road in 13 days in readiness for the 1931 Monza Grand Prix.

*Wind deflecting cowling*

## ▲ THE RECORD-BREAKING "BABS"

A new breed of racer, "Babs" was powered by a 27-litre aeroengine. It raced at Brooklands on many occasions in the 1920s and set a land speed record of 275 kph (171 mph) on Pendine Sands, in 1926.

*Breaker strip to reveal dangerous tyre wear*

*Twin cantilever rear springs*

*7 x 19 in (18 x 48 cm) racing tyres*

## ▶ FASTEST OF ALL

The fastest speed ever recorded at Brooklands was 244.46 kph (151.97 mph). It was attained in 1935 by John Cobb's Napier-Railton, which also holds the lap record of 230.89 kph (143.44 mph). The car was a purpose-built giant, powered by a W12 24-litre Napier Lion aeroengine.

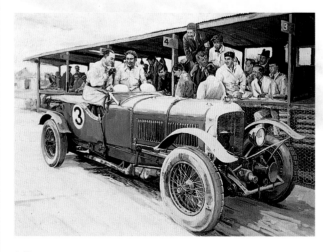

## ▲ SPEED SIX BENTLEY

The Speed Six Bentley won Le Mans in 1929, driven by Woolf Barnato and Sir Henry Birkin. In 1931, with a new 8-litre engine, it crashed over the Brooklands banking.

## ▶ DAZZLING PERFORMANCE

The 100-mph Straker-Squire X2 had a 3.9-litre overhead camshaft engine with six separate cylinders. It was raced at Brooklands in the early 1920s by Bertie Kensington-Moir.

## ▲ ITALIAN THOROUGHBRED

Developed from the 8C2300 Alfa Romeo by the Scuderia Ferrari production team, the "Monza" 8C2600 was a highly successful racer at Brooklands.

*Aeroscreen*

*Quick-release filler cap*

## ◀ THE ZEPPELIN-ENGINED RACING CAR

This Chitty-Chitty-Bang-Bang I, built for racing at Brooklands, was powered by a huge 23-litre Zeppelin aeroengine. It was raced by its owner, the Polish-American Count Louis Vorow Zborowski.

## ◀ FRENCH CONTENDER

Complex but brilliant, the twin-cam straight-eight 1.5-litre Delage won every Grand Prix in the 1927 season, including the British Grand Prix at Brooklands.

*No front brakes*

## BROOKLANDS

The world's first purpose-built racing circuit was a 30-metre (100-foot) wide track forming a huge amphitheatre almost 4.8 km (3 miles) in circumference. Cars raced the Brooklands circuit without effort at 193 kph (120 mph) thanks to 9.1-metre (30-foot) high banked curves.

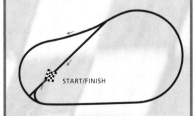

START/FINISH

*Beam front axle located by radius rods*

# 1920-1940 Bugatti Type 35

*PETROL GAUGE*

JUDGED BY MANY to be the most beautiful racing car of all time, the straight-eight Type 35 Bugatti made its debut at the August 1924 Lyons Grand Prix. The car here is one of the five-car Lyons team, and was driven by Pierre de Vizcaya, who had to retire after skidding into a house, bending the car's chassis and rear axle. Produced in engine capacities up to 2.3 litres, and available to any purchaser who could afford the asking price, the Type 35 was especially popular among wealthy sporting amateurs. Its basic price of £1,250 would have paid for a substantial detached house in the London suburbs.

### ▼ STRESS-RELATED CHASSIS

Concealed from sight by the louvred undertray, the chassis of the Type 35 Bugatti varied in vertical section according to the stress imposed on it. The very first T35 Bugattis also featured wooden infills in the front dumbirons.

### ▲ RECORD SUCCESS

The T35 Bugatti was one of the most successful cars in racing history, with a claimed 2,000 victories to its credit between 1924 and 1931, ranging from local hill climbs and sprints to Grands Prix.

*Fuel filler*

*Aeroscreen*

*Gear lever*

*Radius rod*

*Detachable rim*

*Cast-aluminium wheel incorporating brake drum*

*Louvred undertray*

*Handbrake*

Horseshoe-shaped radiator

FRONT VIEW

SIDE VIEW

Vented tail

REAR VIEW

## SPECIFICATION

| | |
|---|---|
| Chassis | tapered channel steel |
| Engine | 2.0-litre straight-eight unsupercharged (T35) |
| | 2.0-litre straight-eight supercharged (T35C) |
| | 2.3-litre straight-eight unsupercharged (T35T) |
| | 2.3-litre straight-eight supercharged (T35B) |
| Valve type | two inlet, one exhaust; single overhead camshaft |
| Transmission | four-speed and reverse |
| Power output | 90–135 bhp |
| Weight | 750 kg (1,654 lb) |
| Suspension | semi-elliptic leaf (front) reversed quarter-elliptic leaf (rear) |
| Top speed | 200 kph (125 mph) |
| Fuel | petrol |

### ▶ LUCKY HORSESHOE

Ettore Bugatti described his lovely Type 35 as a "thoroughbred", and it is said that his love of horses is reflected in the horseshoe shape of the radiator. In plan view, the T35 reveals that its body is shaped like a racing aerofoil.

Aerodynamic shape

TOP VIEW

Dumbirons with wooden infill

Rev counter

Distributor cap

Clock

Advance/retard lever

Air pump for fuel tank

### ◀ BRIGHT SPARK

An unconventional feature of the Bugatti's damascened aluminium dashboard was the exposed distributor cap of the car's ignition magneto.

Oil gauge

Rev counter drive

Drive from camshaft to magneto

Straight-eight engine

Solex carburettor

Conduit for spark-plug leads

Temperature gauge

Stoneguard

Retaining nut

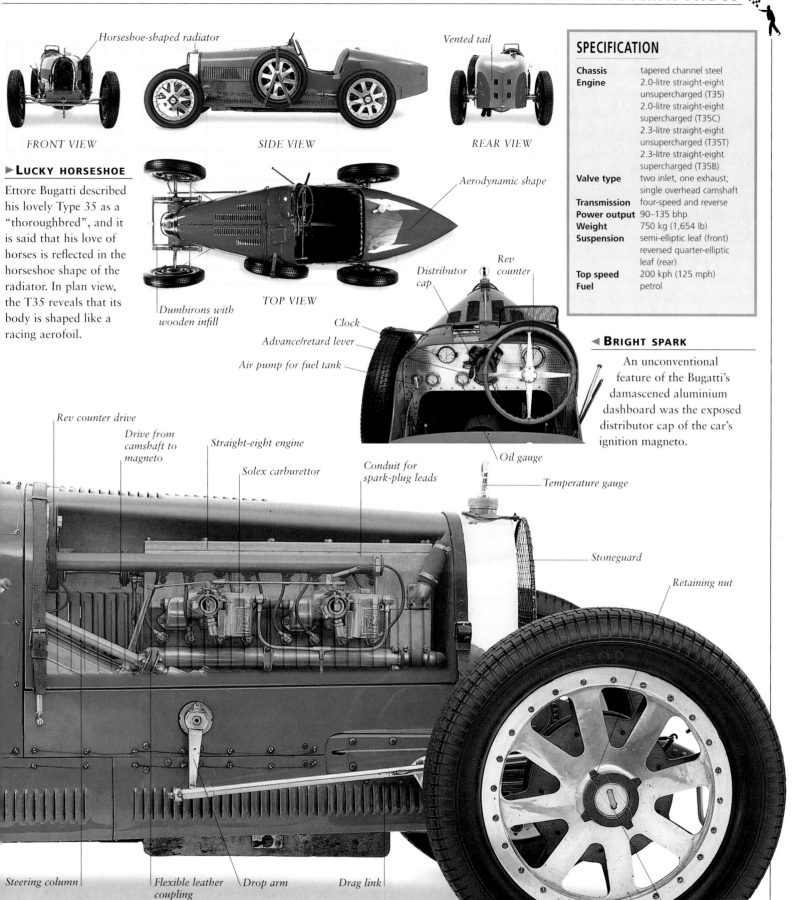

Steering column

Flexible leather coupling

Drop arm

Drag link

Dust cap

# 1920-1940 American Board Tracks

SOUVENIR RACE PROGRAMME

BOARD TRACKS WERE a spectacular feature of the golden age of American racing cars between 1910 and the early 1930s. They were banked oval circuits, up to 3.5 km (2 miles) long, made up of thousands of wooden planks set on edge. The first track was built at Playa del Rey, California, in 1910, and by the 1920s there were tracks all over the United States. Home-grown cars dominated the races, with the rivalry between Duesenberg and Miller a constant feature. However, there were occasional victories for French cars, such as Peugeot and Ballot.

Exhaust system

### ▲ ITALIAN RACER

The 1913 Tipo IM Isotta Fraschini was in many respects typical of the cars that raced on the West Coast. Its distinctive features were its front-wheel brakes and huge drainpipe exhaust.

### ► EARLY LEADER

The eight-cylinder 4.8-litre Duesenberg was the dominant car of the early 1920s. Duesenbergs were victorious in eight out of 11 major board track races in 1920.

Outside gear and brake levers

Friction shock absorbers

Streamlined dumbirons

Chassis tie bar

### ▲ BUILT FOR THE SPEEDWAYS

The French company Ballot built this straight-eight twin-cam racer for the American tracks. In 1922, Ralph de Palma drove this car to victory in an 80-km (50-mile) race on the Beverly Hills board track at over 170 kph (107 mph).

Wind-deflecting cowl

### ◄ KING OF THE BOARD TRACKS

Harry Miller designed this supercharged 1.5-litre Miller 91 which became the king of the board tracks. Miller had shot to fame when a Duesenberg with one of his straight-eight 183-cu in engines won the 1922 Indianapolis 500 at record speed.

Undershield

### ► MILLER DOMINANCE

The dominance of the Miller racers in the mid-1920s can be seen from this picture of the Culver City track, where they occupy three of the first four places. Culver City was one of the few financial failures, opening in 1924 $250,000 in debt and lasting only four years.

## ▲ FRENCH CONNECTION

Duesenberg won the 1921 French Grand Prix, and later that year Harry Hartz raced this 3-litre car from the winning team on the Beverly Hills board track. The car still has the French licence number on its tail.

## ▲ MODEL T FORD'S FAST SISTER

This 1922 Fronty-Ford was powered by a highly-modified Model T Ford engine which was fitted with a "Frontenac" overhead-valve conversion by Louis Chevrolet.

*Radiator temperature gauge*

*Steel disc wheels for strength*

*Engine set back for balance*

*Exposed petrol tank*

## ◄ WEST-COAST FLYER

Faster than its rival Peugeots, this 7.4-litre Mercer 450 took Eddie Pullen to victory in the 1914 American Grand Prix at Corona, California. Pullen drove over 480 km (300 miles) at an average speed of 140.5 kph (87.4 mph).

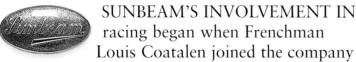

# 1920-1940 The Sunbeam Marque

SUNBEAM'S INVOLVEMENT IN racing began when Frenchman Louis Coatalen joined the company as chief engineer in 1909. He realized that success in motor sport was crucial as a way of presenting Sunbeam cars to the public. Over the next 20 years, Sunbeam became a household name for their successes in various competitions, from road racing – particularly the Tourist Trophy race run around the Isle of Man – to the land speed record. When Sunbeam withdrew from motor racing during the economic depression of the early 1930s, their demise as an independent company soon followed.

## ▲ SIMPLE SUCCESS STORY

Built for the 1912 Coupe de l'Auto race, held over a 65-km (47-mile) circuit near Dieppe, France, this 3-litre Sunbeam was later adapted as a road car. The race was a great success for these uncomplicated sidevalve four-cylinder cars which finished first, second, and third.

## ▶ AEROENGINED MONSTER

The mighty 350 hp Sunbeam, with its 18.3-litre V12 engine, set a new land speed record of 215 kph (133.75 mph) at Brooklands in 1922, driven by Kenelm Lee Guinness.

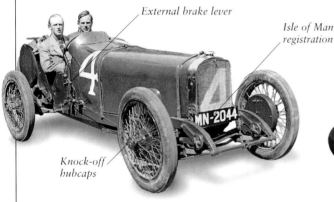

*External brake lever*

*Isle of Man registration*

*Long tail to keep car steady at top speed*

*Knock-off hubcaps*

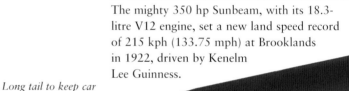

## ▲ TOURIST-TROPHY VICTOR

Henry Segrave drove one of the 3-litre Sunbeam cars entered for the 1922 Isle of Man Tourist Trophy. Their twin-cam straight-eight engines made them the fastest cars in the race, and Segrave's team-mate, Jean Chassagne, had a winning margin of over four minutes.

## ▼ HOLD THAT TIGER

The 4-litre V12 Sunbeam Tiger, originally built for the 1926 Grand Prix season, achieved many successes in racing and record-breaking. In 1928 it won the Gold Star handicap at Brooklands, and the winning speed of 206.4 kph (128.36 mph) was a track record.

## ▲ GOOD FOR GUINNESS

Kenelm Lee Guinness, one of Sunbeam's leading drivers, briefly led the 1924 French Grand Prix at Lyons with his six-cylinder supercharged Sunbeam. Guinness was forced to retire when a bearing failed in his car's transmission.

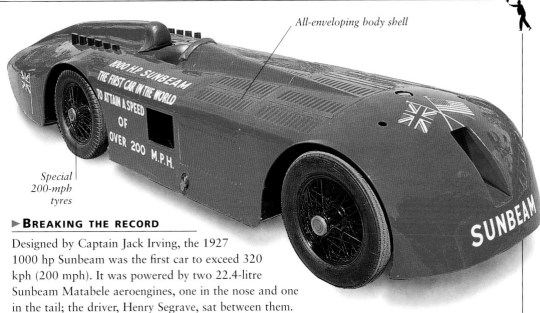

*All-enveloping body shell*

*Special 200-mph tyres*

### ▲ TOODLES GOES TO INDY

The first British car to race at Indianapolis was this 1911 6.1-litre six-cylinder record-breaker "Toodles IV", which finished fourth in the 1913 race, driven by Albert Guyot. "Toodles" was Sunbeam engineer Louis Coatalen's pet name for his wife, Olive.

### ▶ BREAKING THE RECORD

Designed by Captain Jack Irving, the 1927 1000 hp Sunbeam was the first car to exceed 320 kph (200 mph). It was powered by two 22.4-litre Sunbeam Matabele aeroengines, one in the nose and one in the tail; the driver, Henry Segrave, sat between them.

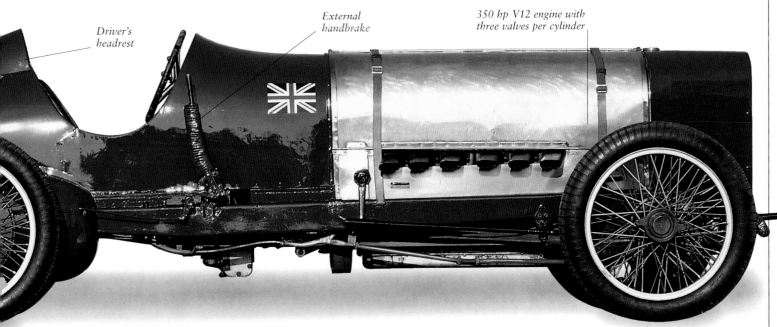

*Driver's headrest*

*External handbrake*

*350 hp V12 engine with three valves per cylinder*

*Aerodynamic radiator cowling*

### RACING HIGHLIGHTS

**1910** Sunbeam's first racing car is the cigar-shaped *Nautilus*, unveiled at Brooklands

**1912** Victory for the 3-litre Sunbeams in the Coupe de l'Auto in France

**1913** Sunbeam's 9-litre record breaker *Toodles V* is the world's first V12 car

**1914** A 3.3-litre Sunbeam wins the Isle of Man Tourist Trophy race

**1922** Another Tourist Trophy victory for a 3-litre Sunbeam, driven by Jean Chassagne

**1923** A 2-litre Sunbeam wins the French Grand Prix

**1924** Malcolm Campbell sets a new land speed record of 235.28 kph (146.16 mph) with the 350 hp Sunbeam

**1927** The 1000 hp Sunbeam is the first car to exceed 320 kph (200 mph)

### ▼ THE CUB AT BROOKLANDS

This supercharged 2-litre six-cylinder Sunbeam was originally built for the 1924 Grand Prix but was later developed for track racing as "The Cub". It could lap Brooklands at 200 kph (125 mph).

*Aeroscreen*

*Straight-through exhaust pipe*

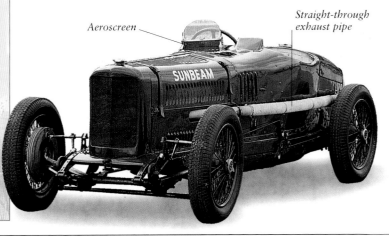

# 1920-1940 The Montlhéry Autodrome

*DELAGE ON THE BANKING*

BUILT AT A cost of £500,000 in 1924 by newspaper proprietor and radiator manufacturer, Lamblin, the Montlhéry Autodrome was France's rival to Brooklands in England. Its mighty ferroconcrete banking rose up alongside the main Paris-Orleans road like a modern-day Colosseum. It was a fitting arena for the contests between Delage and Bugatti which were a feature of racing in the 1920s. Montlhéry first staged the French Grand Prix in 1925, and for much of the 1930s it was the venue for this race. Montlhéry also hosted sports-car races such as the Grand Prix du Salon, for road cars rather than racing cars.

### ▲ SPEEDY SALMSON

The highlight of the opening meeting at Montlhéry in 1924 was a 200-km (124-mile) race for light cars of up to 1100cc engine capacity. The race attracted an entry largely made up of Salmsons; and the winner, this twin-cam 1.1-litre model, had an average speed of over 136 kph (85mph).

### ▲ RECORD-BREAKING MONSTER

This huge 9.1-litre Renault 45 was a famous record-breaker at Montlhéry. In 1925 it was the first car to be driven in excess of 160 kph (100 mph) over a continuous 24-hour period, averaging almost 174 kph (108 mph).

*Delahaye 135*

*Ventilation louvres*

*Engine-turned aluminium body*

### ▶ COMPLEX BUT EFFECTIVE

The 2 LCV 2-litre V12 Delage was a complex but effective Grand Prix car. In the 1925 French Grand Prix, it was up against the Italian Alfa Romeo team. The Italians withdrew, however, after the death of their driver, Antonio Ascari, and the Delage of Albert Divo won.

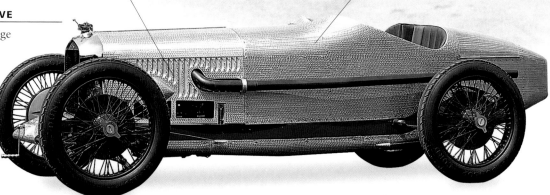

## ▲ WHEEL CHANGE

Knock-off hubcaps were invented by Peugeot in 1913 to speed up wheel-changing. This is one of the Talbot-Darracq team, which finished first, second, third, and fifth in the Sports Car Grand Prix of 1937.

*albot-Darracq*

## ▼ LIGHTWEIGHT THOROUGHBRED

Bugatti's great rival on the 1920s racetracks was the C6 Amilcar. This potent 1100cc twin-cam six-cylinder model could produce up to 108 bhp in supercharged form. Amilcar took first, second, and third place in its class in the 1925 Grand Prix du Salon at Montlhéry.

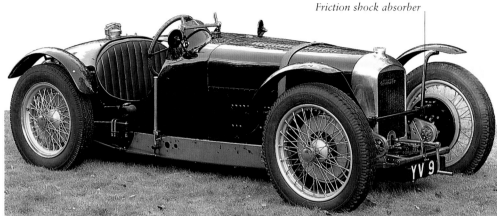

*Friction shock absorber*

## ▲ TALBOT'S CHALLENGE

William Grover-Williams drove this eight-cylinder 1.5-litre Talbot in the 1927 French Grand Prix. Like every other championship race of that season, it was a Delage victory, but Williams' Talbot came fourth despite fuel starvation.

*Lagonda 4.5-litre*

## ▲ SPORTS CAR GRAND PRIX

The 1936 French Grand Prix was restricted to sports cars – ordinary road cars rather than specialized racers – to ensure a French winner after a crushing defeat by Mercedes in 1935. The ploy worked, and a French-built streamlined Bugatti T57G duly won.

## ▼ SCIENCE FICTION ON WHEELS

This futuristic Voisin, a star of the 1998 "Vintage Montlhéry Lalique" revival meeting, was designed for the 1923 Tours Grand Prix by aviation-pioneer-turned-motor-manufacturer Gabriel Voisin. It was the first monocoque Grand Prix car, with chassis and body as a single unit.

*Crab-track rear wheels*

*Monocoque body*

*Airscrew-driven water pump*

### MONTLHÉRY

START/FINISH

As well as its fast 2.6-km (1.6-mile) banked oval, Montlhéry incorporated a series of interlinked road circuits. This could create a longest lap of 12.5 km (7.8 miles), and made the Montlhéry autodrome an ideal venue for all kinds of racing and record-breaking events.

# 1920-1940 Miller 91

ENGINEERING GENIUS Harry Miller's masterpiece was the Miller 91, designed for the new 1.5-litre supercharged international racing formula that came into force in 1926. Its twin-cam straight-eight power unit became known as the "little engine", because of the compact elegance of its construction. Nonetheless it could be readily tuned to produce 230 bhp. Jimmy Murphy recorded a two-way average of 262 kph (164 mph) on California's Muroc Dry Lake in a Miller 91 in 1927, touching a speed of 275 kph (171 mph) in one direction. At the time, the land speed record, set by a 44-litre twin-engined car, was only 53 kph (33 mph) higher. Ettore Bugatti was amazed by the Miller's performance, and copied its twin-cam technology.

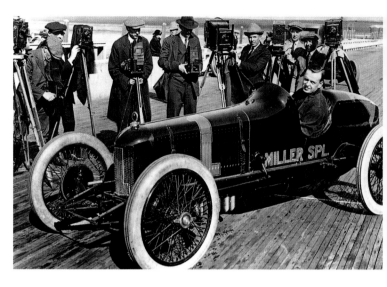

### ▲ STAR OF THE SILENT SCREEN

The Miller was undisputed king of the board tracks in the 1920s. This example is being admired by photographers at the circuit at Culver City, which was adjacent to a film studio.

### ▶ GOLDEN CAR OF THE GOLDEN AGE

This beautiful gold-painted 91 was driven to victory in the 1928 Indianapolis 500 by Louis Meyer, whose winning average was close to 160 kph (100 mph), a world-class record. Meyer went on to become the first three-times winner of the Indianapolis 500.

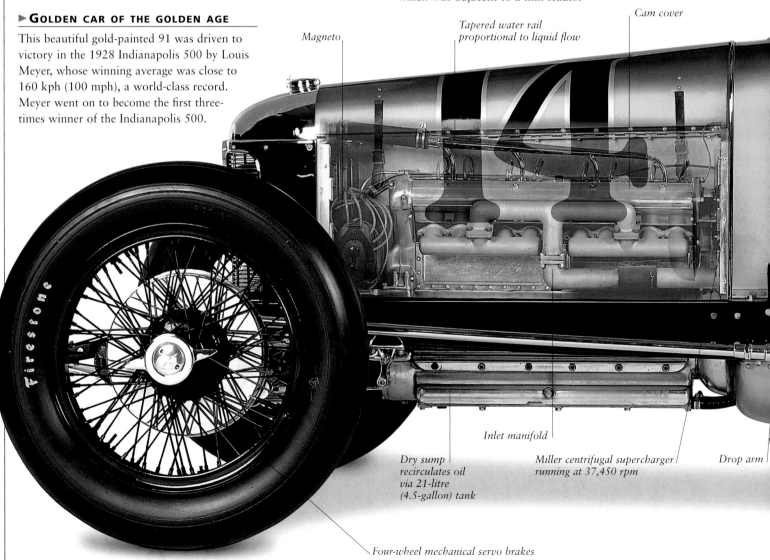

Magneto

Tapered water rail proportional to liquid flow

Cam cover

Inlet manifold

Dry sump recirculates oil via 21-litre (4.5-gallon) tank

Miller centrifugal supercharger running at 37,450 rpm

Drop arm

Four-wheel mechanical servo brakes

FRONT VIEW

Nickel-plated radiator shield

Handbrake

Straight-through exhaust

Body shaped to fit driver

SIDE VIEW

REAR VIEW

Filler aperture for dry sump oiling system

Semi-elliptic Leaf springs

Starting handle

TOP VIEW

## ▶ FUNCTIONAL AND FORM-FITTING

A golden car from a golden age: the beautiful lines of the Miller 91 were drawn up by master draughtsman Leo Goossen. The elegant body fitted snugly round the driver and weighed a mere 34.4 kg (76 lb).

### SPECIFICATION

| | |
|---|---|
| Chassis | mild steel channel |
| Engine | 1.5-litre straight-eight supercharged |
| Valve type | one inlet, one exhaust; two overhead camshafts |
| Transmission | three-speed and reverse |
| Power output | 230 bhp |
| Weight | 635 kg (1,400 lb) |
| Suspension | semi-elliptic leaf (front) semi-elliptic leaf (rear) |
| Top speed | 275 kph (171 mph) |
| Fuel | leaded petrol/benzol mix or methanol |

## ▶ PERFECTIONIST FINISH

Simple yet elegant, the aluminium dash of the Miller 91 reflects the perfectionist standards of Harry Miller and his loyal team of craftsmen.

Boost gauge

Tachometer

Cutaway steering wheel

Wind-deflecting cowl

Detachable cockpit trim

Cord-bound steering wheel

Channel steel chassis

Undershield

Firestone speedway tyres

Triple-laced wire lock-ring wheel

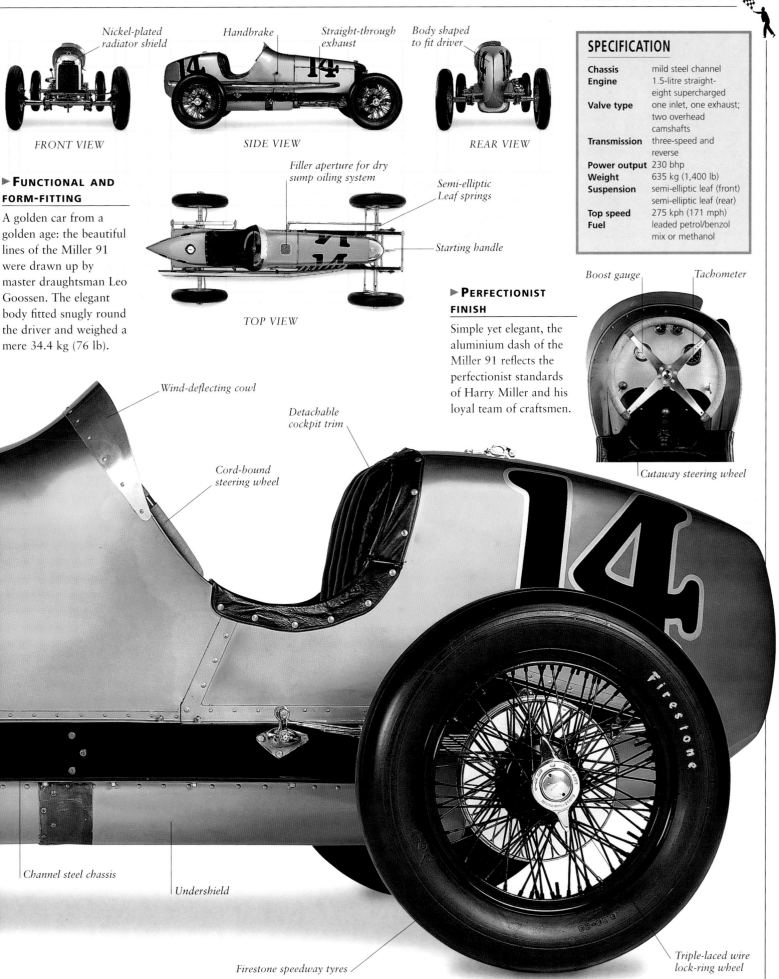

# 1920-1940 The Mille Miglia

**1000 MIGLIA >**

THE LAST OF the great road races was the Italian Mille Miglia. The race was the brainchild of Count Aymo Maggi, who wanted to make his home town of Brescia the focus of the world's greatest road race. Starting and finishing at Brescia, the Mille Miglia covered a thousand uncompromising miles through the Italian countryside. The race was a showpiece for all of the important Italian marques: Alfa Romeo, Fiat, Maserati, and Isotta. However, road-racing became increasingly dangerous after World War II, and the Mille Miglia was finally banned after a tragic crash in 1957.

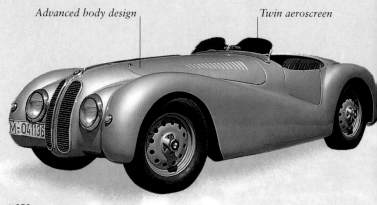

*Advanced body design*  *Twin aeroscreen*

## ▲ WARTIME WINNER

The 1940 Mille Miglia was won by this BMW 328, driven by Baron Huschke von Hanstein. Specially built for the race, and powered by a 2-litre engine, the car's streamlined body influenced the styling of postwar cars such as the Jaguar XK120.

## ▲ FOUNDER'S CAR

Count Aymo Maggi, nobleman and racing driver, started first in the 1927 Mille Miglia in his Isotta Fraschini 8A SS. This four-seater sports tourer was powered by a 7.3-litre straight-eight engine, and was capable of 160 kph (100 mph).

*Transparent headlamp covers*

## ◄ SECOND TIME ROUND

This 8C2300MM Alfa Romeo, part of the Ferrari team, had its engine uprated from 2.3 litres to 2.6 litres for the Mille Miglia of 1933. The car was driven by Tazio Nuvolari, who achieved his second victory in this race. The Ferrari team cars had transparent covers over the headlamps that were colour-coded for night-time identification.

*"Monza" radiator cowl*

## ▶ DREAM TEAM

The "Alfa Corse" racing team, directed by Enzo Ferrari, featured 8C2900 Alfa Romeo Spyders. Their straight-eight twin-cam engines gave a top speed of 185 kph (116 mph), and the cars were driven by some of Italy's best drivers.

## ▼ FAST AND FURIOUS

This 8C2900A Alfa Romeo, which won the Mille Miglia in 1936, was a thinly disguised Grand Prix racer fitted with a two-seater body. The race was meant for standard touring cars, but the winners were often specialist racing cars.

*Folding windscreen*

## ▲ AERODYNAMIC SALOON

The little Fiat Balilla of 1933 to 1937 was a sporting overhead-valve derivative of the popular 995cc Tipo 508 family saloon car. This racing version was a favourite among amateur competitors.

## ▼ FAILED TO FINISH

In the 1928 Mille Miglia, Aymo Maggi drove this straight-eight 1.5-litre Maserati, with Ernesto Maserati as co-driver. Having the car's maker on board was no guarantee of success, and the hand-built two-seater capable of 160 kph(100 mph), was out of the race before it reached Rome.

*Cutaway wings*

## ▲ HIGH FLYER

A 2.6-litre 8C2600 Alfa Romeo Monza two-seater negotiates the Futa and Raticosa Passes between Bologna and Florence. This mountain crossing was the most spectacular section of the Mille Miglia course.

# 1920-1940 Alfa Romeo 8C2300

BONNET
BADGE

LAUNCHED IN 1931 to counter the new sports racers from such rival marques as Bugatti and Mercedes-Benz, the supercharged twin-overhead camshaft 8C2300 was designed by the talented Vittorio Jano, who had been recruited from Fiat to design Alfa's racing cars. The Scuderia Ferrari, Alfa Romeo's racing department which was run by Enzo Ferrari, uprated the engine of these very special racers to 2.6 litres. The model's debut in the 1931 Mille Miglia proved a disappointment, but after that it was virtually invincible, winning the Targa Florio three years in succession from 1931, Le Mans four times in succession from the same year, and the Mille Miglia in 1932, 1933, and 1934.

▲ **DIFFICULT DEBUT**

The most famous Alfa Romeo ace, Tazio Nuvolari, awaits the start of the 1931 Mille Miglia in an early 8C2300 "Spider Corsa" (a racing two-seater) on a short wheelbase chassis. Despite crashing into a milestone and damaging the oil tank, he finished eighth.

▶ **DUAL-PURPOSE MUDGUARDS**

The elegant mudguards on this Touring Alfa Romeo are designed to offer minimum wind resistance. The idea of storing the battery and tools in streamlined boxes formed out of the regulation running boards was brilliant.

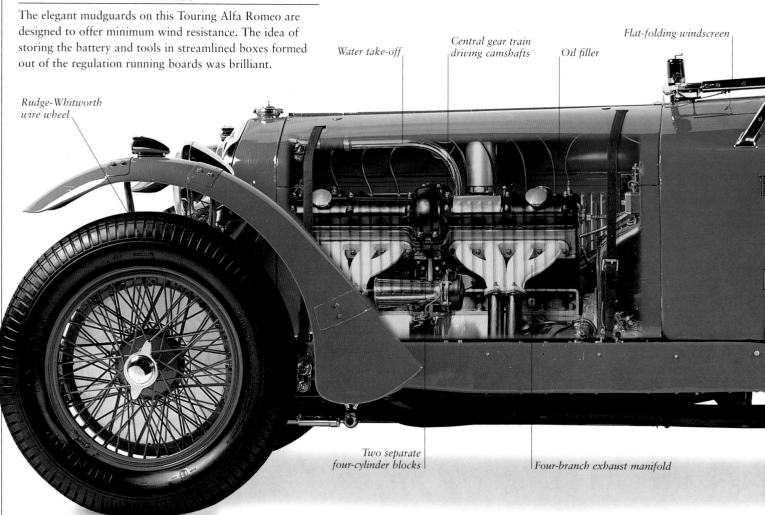

Rudge-Whitworth
wire wheel

Water take-off

Central gear train
driving camshafts

Oil filler

Flat-folding windscreen

Two separate
four-cylinder blocks

Four-branch exhaust manifold

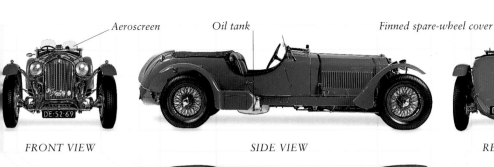

Aeroscreen    Oil tank    Finned spare-wheel cover

*FRONT VIEW*    *SIDE VIEW*    *REAR VIEW*

## SPECIFICATION

| | |
|---|---|
| Chassis | mild-steel channel |
| Engine | 2.3-litre straight-eight supercharged |
| Valve type | one inlet, one exhaust; two overhead camshafts |
| Transmission | four-speed and reverse |
| Power output | 165-180 bhp |
| Weight | 1,000 kg (2,200 lb) |
| Suspension | semi-elliptic leaf (front) semi-elliptic leaf (rear) |
| Top speed | 215 kph (140 mph) |
| Fuel | petrol |

### ▶ CLASSIC TOURER

The bodywork of the Le Mans version of the Alfa Romeo 8C2300 was made by Italy's most celebrated sporting coachbuilder, Touring of Milan. The car conformed to the original Le Mans regulations, which required cars over 1100cc to be fitted with four-seat bodywork.

*TOP VIEW*

Fairing over dumbirons

Streamlined mudguard

### ▶ FULLY INSTRUMENTED

The businesslike instrument board of the Alfa Romeo 8C2300 provides the driver with the fullest possible information.

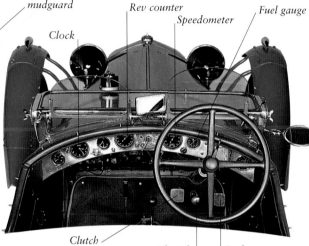

Rev counter    Speedometer    Fuel gauge

Clock

Clutch    Throttle    Brake

— Aeroscreen

Leather cover for regulation rear seats

Steering wheel

Streamlined battery box integral with wings

Fishtail exhaust

Knock-off hubcap

# The Auto Union Marque

**1920-1940**

THE FIRST MARQUE to achieve success in motor sport with rear-engined cars, the Germany-based Auto Union company was formed in 1932 by the fusion of Audi, DKW, Horch, and Wanderer. Encouraged by the newly elected Nazi regime, Auto Union took up motor racing with the P-Wagen, designed by Ferdinand Porsche in 1934 for the new formula for cars weighing less than 750 kg (1,650 lb). With a mid-mounted 4.4-litre V16 engine and a five-speed gearbox, the Auto Union was a design decades ahead of its time. Auto Union and Mercedes held sway on the racing circuits of the 1930s much as Bugatti had done in the 1920s.

**▲ WINNER IN ITALY**

Italy's top driver Tazio Nuvolari joined the Auto Union team in 1938, driving the new 3-litre Type D, with its V12 power unit. To the joy of local fans, he won the Italian Grand Prix. "German engine, Italian heart," they cheered.

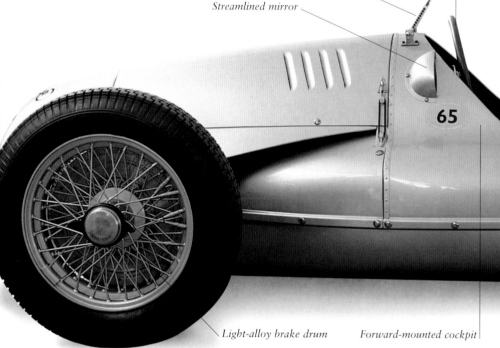

Folding aeroscreen

Streamlined mirror

Steering wheel

65

Light-alloy brake drum          Forward-mounted cockpit

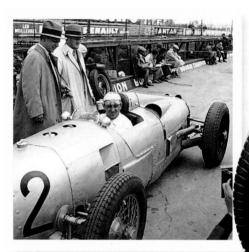

**▲ AEROPLANE ON WHEELS**

The 1934 Type A Auto Union was described as looking "like an aeroplane fuselage on wheels, finished in frail aluminium and covered with air scoops and vents". This is the reserve car for the 1934 French Grand Prix at Montlhéry.

**◀ BANKING ON SUCCESS**

Auto Union made a spectacular debut at the banked Berlin AVUS track in 1934 when Hans Stuck set new 100-mile (160-km) and 200-km (125-mile) records, at an average speed of 217 kph (134.9 mph).

**▼ IMPROVED DESIGN**

For 1935, an improved Type B made its appearance, with 16 vertical exhaust stubs replacing the twin tailpipes. The car had aluminium side panels instead of the doped aircraft fabric that was used in 1934. The engine size was increased to 5 litres.

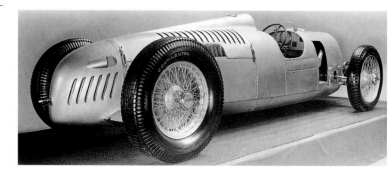

## ▶ DR PORSCHE'S FINALE

The 6.1-litre Type C Auto Union was the last of the company's Grand Prix cars to be designed by Dr Ferdinand Porsche. Its three-cam V16 power unit took driver Bernd Rosemeyer to victory in five Grands Prix.

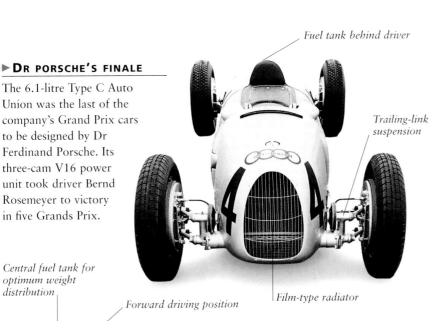

Fuel tank behind driver

Trailing-link suspension

Central fuel tank for optimum weight distribution

Forward driving position

Film-type radiator

Stub exhausts

Lateral fuel tank extension

## ▲ STREAMLINER

Bernd Rosemeyer's streamlined Auto Union speeds round the Berlin AVUS in 1937. This 6.3-litre car had extra engine-cooling inlets cut into its wings. On the brick-paved track's 10-km (6-mile) straights, the Auto Union streamliners could reach almost 385 kph (240 mph).

## ◀ EASIER TO DRIVE

With its pannier fuel tanks and single-stage supercharged V12 power unit, the 1938 Type D Auto Union offered better handling than its predecessors.

19 in (48 cm) rear wheels for normal circuits, 22 in (56 cm) for fast circuits

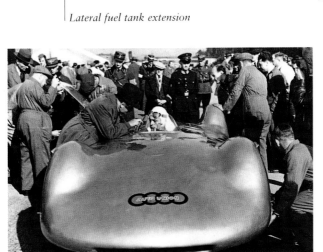

## ◀ FASTEST ON THE ROAD

Auto Union's Bernd Rosemeyer is seated at the wheel of a 6.3-litre streamliner. In October 1937 Auto Union and Mercedes competed to be the first past the 400 kph (250 mph) barrier on a stretch of Reichsautobahn, the state highway between Frankfurt and Darmstadt. The honour went to Rosemeyer.

### RACING HIGHLIGHTS

| | |
|---|---|
| 1934 | First racing victory for the new Type A is the German Grand Prix |
| 1935 | Improved Type B Auto Unions win Italian, Tunis, and Czech Grands Prix and the Coppa Acerbo |
| 1936 | Bernd Rosemeyer in a Type C wins Eifel, German, Pescara, Swiss, and Italian Grands Prix, and the European Championship |
| 1937 | Rudi Hasse wins Belgian Grand Prix, while Bernd Rosemeyer takes Eifel Grand Prix, Vanderbilt Cup, Coppa Acerbo, and Donington Grand Prix, all victories for the Type C Auto Union |
| 1938 | Tazio Nuvolari wins Italian and Donington Grands Prix in the Type D Auto Union |
| 1939 | Nuvolari wins the last Grand Prix before World War II in Czechoslovakia |

# 1920-1940 The Nürburgring Grand Prix

*1934 GRAND PRIX POSTER*

THE NORDSCHLIEFE (North Loop) of the classic Nürburgring was one of the most awesome tests that could be offered to the cars and drivers of the 1930s. Built in the mid-1920s to create work for the unemployed, the Nürburgring circuit included the celebrated steeply banked Karussell curve.

The track was the venue for some of the most exciting races of the 1930s, when the state-backed Mercedes and Auto Union teams vied for supremacy. Enormous crowds of up to 350,000 people attended the German Grand Prix during the 1930s, and victory for the German cars was a matter of national pride.

### ▶ ENGLISHMAN ABROAD

Englishman Dick Seaman acknowledges the cheers of the crowd with a half-hearted salute after his historic victory in the 1938 German Grand Prix with one of the new W154 V12 Mercedes. Seaman joined Mercedes in 1937 but was killed in a crash in the 1939 Belgian Grand Prix.

### ▼ ALL CHANGE

Herman Lang drove this W25C Mercedes in the 1936 German Grand Prix at the Nürburgring. The car's eight-cylinder 4.3-litre engine could generate 445 hp. Lang managed seventh place in spite of having to swap cars and suffering a broken finger during the race.

*Maserati 8CM*

*Radiator filler*

*External oil pipes*

### ▲ UNEQUAL STRUGGLE

Tazio Nuvolari drove a 2.6-litre straight-eight Tipo B Alfa Romeo in the 1935 German Grand Prix. Even though his car was outclassed in comparison with the mighty Mercedes "Silver Arrows" cars, Nuvolari's driving skills snatched victory on the last lap.

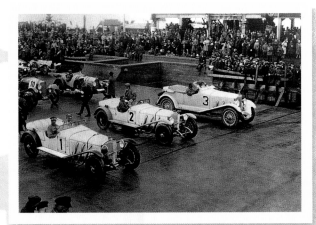

## ▲ SPORTS CARS

The first Grand Prix at the Nürburgring in 1927 was confined to sports cars. Two of the front three cars on the grid were vast supercharged 6.8-litre S-Type Mercedes, which finished first and second.

## ▼ TWO LEGENDS MEET

This surviving 5.7-litre Mercedes Benz W125, driven at the Goodward Festival of Speed by British ex-World Champion John Surtees, still has the capacity to thrill. This car was a successful racer at the Nürburgring in the 1930s.

## ▼ MERCEDES WIN

Dick Seaman is on the way to victory at the wheel of a W154 V12 Mercedes during the 1938 German Grand Prix. "I only wish it had been a British car," the English driver was later heard to remark.

*8C2300 Alfa Romeo Monza*

*T35 Bugatti*

*Mercedes W25 "Silver Arrow"*

## NÜRBURGRING

Forming a wide loop around the Nürburg mountain, the Nürburgring was an awesome test of driving skill. Each lap of its 22.5-km (14-mile) circuit required drivers to negotiate a total of 174 bends. These included the Karussell, where the fastest drivers used the ditch on the inside of the bend as a banking which was eventually paved.

START/FINISH

## ▲ FIRST OF THE SILVER ARROWS

The 1934 Grand Prix included a seven-year-old Bugatti and eight Alfa Romeos. This was the first season for the new Mercedes W25 "Silver Arrows", whose aluminium bodies were left unpainted to squeeze them under the new 750 kg (15 cwt) maximum weight.

# 1920-1940 The Mercedes Marque

THE MERCEDES MARQUE made a victorious debut at the 1901 Nice Automobile Week, and became a dominant force in motor sport. During the 1930s, the company's Silver Arrows – so-called because the cars were left unpainted to reduce their weight – were almost unbeatable. The new generation of Silver Arrows in the 1950s proved that the company had lost none of its technological leadership. After a terrible crash at Le Mans in 1955, Mercedes dropped out of motor sport until 1988, when the company teamed up with Sauber. Mercedes went on to team up with McLaren to win the 1998 drivers' and constructors' championship.

**◀ FRENCH WINNER**

The first shaft-driven racer to come from the Mercedes works at Stuttgart-Unterturkheim was the 4.5-litre car which won the 1914 French Grand Prix. Its four-cylinder engine had a single overhead camshaft, with two valves and four spark plugs per cylinder.

*Pointed honeycomb radiator*

*Driver's protective windscreen*

*Torsion-bar-sprung De Dion suspension*

**▲ MOUNTAIN VEHICLE**

This chain-driven 80 hp Mercedes was built for the 1907 Kaiserpreis race, a contest sponsored by Kaiser Wilhelm II and run over a course in the Taunus mountains. The car finished ninth, driven by Otto Salzer.

**▶ MIGHTY GIANT**

The new W125 built for the 1937 season featured a twin-tube chassis with De Dion rear suspension and a 5.7-litre engine developing 646 hp.

**▼ SUPERCHARGED RACER**

This 2-litre supercharged Mercedes won the 1924 Coppa Florio race. Mercedes' experience with building aeroengines gave them a head start in designing supercharged cars.

**▲ RACING AGAINST THE TIDE**

This 12.8-litre Mercedes belonged to the sugar magnate A.W. Tate, who raced it on the sands at Saltburn in Lancashire. Examples of this Mercedes model enjoyed several years' racing in Britain and America after its win at the 1908 Grand Prix at Dieppe.

## SOUTH AMERICA WAY

Mercedes' supercharging skills enabled them to build big, brutal sports cars in the 1920s, like this 7.1-litre six-cylinder SSK which was raced in Argentina by Carlos Zatuszek in 1931.

*Twin headrests*

*Air intake*

## MILLE WINNER

Developed from the W196 Grand Prix Mercedes, the eight-cylinder 300SLR was the world champion sportscar of 1955. The car shown here achieved legendary status when Stirling Moss drove it to victory in the 1955 Mille Miglia in Italy.

## THE GULLWING

The 300SL endurance racing prototype of 1952 had an ingenious multitube spaceframe chassis. The car also featured gullwing doors which opened upwards. Victory at Le Mans and in the Carrera Panamericana paved the way for a fuel-injected production version.

*Gullwing door*

*Main air intake for radiator*

*Auxiliary air intake*

*Coil and wishbone independent suspension*

## MERCEDES' RETURN

The 1990 Sauber-Mercedes C11 was one of the cars built after Mercedes' return to motor sport in 1988. Mercedes gave backing to the Sauber team, whose endurance cars were powered by 5-litre twin-turbocharged V8 engines. In 1989 Sauber-Mercedes finished first and second at Le Mans.

*Fin to control airflow*

*NACA duct*

### RACING HIGHLIGHTS

| | |
|---|---|
| 1903 | Camille Jenatzy wins the Gordon Bennett race in Ireland in a 60-hp Mercedes |
| 1908 | Christian Lautenschlager's 12.8-litre Mercedes wins the French Grand Prix |
| 1914 | Lautenschlager's 4.5-litre Mercedes heads 1-2-3 win in the French Grand Prix |
| 1914 | Victory for Ralph DePalma's 18/100 Mercedes in the Vanderbilt Cup |
| 1915 | DePalma's 18/100 Mercedes wins the Indianapolis 500 |
| 1926 | Rudi Caracciola's 2-litre straight-eight Mercedes wins the German Grand Prix |
| 1934 | The first victory for the "Silver Arrows" is won by Manfred von Brauchitsch's W25 in the Eifelrennen |
| 1935 | "Silver Arrows" win seven Grands Prix |
| 1952 | Victory at Le Mans for the Mercedes 300SL six-cylinder gullwing |
| 1954 | Mercedes' comeback to Formula 1 racing with the W196 is marked by Juan Fangio winning the world championship |
| 1955 | Six Grand Prix wins for the W196 Mercedes, Fangio's world championship, and Stirling Moss's historic Mille Miglia victory in the 300SLR |
| 1988 | Mercedes return to motor racing, winning the World Sports Car championship in 1989–1990 with the 5-litre Sauber-Mercedes |
| 1998 | Mika Hakkinen's McLaren Mercedes MP4-13 wins the drivers' and constructors' Grand Prix championships |

# 1920-1940 The Monaco Grand Prix

*MONACO POSTER*

BEFORE 1929, GRAND Prix circuits had been located in the countryside or on purpose-built racetracks such as Brooklands or Monza. The first Monaco Grand Prix brought a new dimension to the sport, for it was run round the streets of the principality's capital, Monte Carlo, on a tight, twisting course. The course put a premium on the manoeuvrability of the cars and the skill of the drivers rather than on sheer power. Early Monaco Grands Prix favoured the agile Bugattis, but their run of success was brought to an end by Tazio Nuvolari's Alfa Romeo 8C Monza in 1932.

### ▲ HOT PURSUIT

An unlikely entry for the first Monaco Grand Prix, the 1.5-litre Corre-La Licorne driven by Michel Dore, attempts to shake off a harrying Bugatti. Although Corre had been racing since 1901, the marque's only notable success was victory at the 1930 Monte Carlo rally.

*Scuderia Ferrari emblem*

### ▲ BAD BRAKES

Tazio Nuvolari drove a 3.8-litre 8C-35 Alfa Romeo in the 1936 Monaco Grand Prix. He led the race for 30 laps in almost continuous rain, but fell back with braking problems.

*Double coil spring suspension*

### ▲ TIGHT TURNS

Although it was manifestly unsuitable for the tight curves and narrow roads of Monte Carlo, this 7.1-litre supercharged Mercedes driven by the talented Rudi Caracciola led the 1929 Grand Prix at one stage. It was eventually beaten into third place by the more nimble Bugattis.

## ▼ IDEAL RACER

First seen at the 1933 Tunis Grand Prix, the straight-eight supercharged 3-litre Tipo 8CM Maserati was capable of 240 kph (144 mph), and was ideally suited to the Monaco circuit, particularly in the hands of drivers like Raymond Sommer and "Phi-Phi" Etancelin.

*Bonnet strap*

*Exposed exhaust pipe*

*Fuel filler*

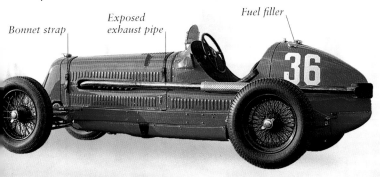

## ▲ LOST CHANCE

Monegasque driver Louis Chiron missed the 1929 Monaco Grand Prix to race at Indianapolis. He returned in 1930, however, in this T35 Bugatti and was leading until he stopped for fuel on the 84th lap, allowing René Dreyfus to win.

## ▶ RACING SUCCESS

The Type 35 Bugatti was available with engines of 1500cc, 2000cc, or 2300cc, to suit various race formulae. The most successful racer of the 1920s, it had over 2,000 victories to its credit, including the very first Monaco Grand Prix.

*Horseshoe-shaped radiator*

*Cast aluminium wheel*

## ▲ CHARIOT RACE

The first Monaco Grand Prix in 1929 attracted an entry of 23 cars, mostly Bugattis. Hailed as "the nearest approach to a Roman chariot race that has been seen of recent years", the event was won by a Type 35 Bugatti driven by William Grover-Williams.

### MONACO

START/FINISH

The first round-the-houses race, the Monaco Grand Prix, put Monte Carlo on the motor-racing map. The course, devised by Anthony Noghès, had a lap distance of less than 3.2 km (2 miles). With the harbour as a spectacular backdrop, the Monaco Grand Prix became one of the most glamorous events in motor racing.

GRAND PRIX d'EUROPE
AUTOS
4
10
E.RUPRECHT
INTERNAT.
MOTORRADRENNEN
BERN 3./4. Juli 1948

# 1940-1960

# A PERIOD OF CHANGE

◀ **RACING
REVIVAL**

The impact of
World War II was
felt far and wide,
even in neutral
Switzerland. After
the war, motor
racing was revived
across Europe.

WORLD WAR II brought a halt to racing in Europe, but once hostilities had ceased the enthusiasts lost no time in resuming their activities, although the old prewar cars had to soldier on for a while due to the shortage of materials. In Britain wartime airfields were surplus to requirements and provided an opportunity for the development of much-needed race circuits. It was a time of bold beginnings. Alongside Italy's established Maserati and Alfa Romeo marques, the new Ferrari sports and racing cars stormed on to the racing scene. They were destined to achieve unprecedented success, urged on by the autocratic Enzo Ferrari, a man who lived for racing alone. Britain at last produced world-beating Grand Prix cars and the BRM was established. It was built to break Italy's stranglehold on Grand Prix racing but was never quite able to deliver the goods. The period saw revolutionary designs heading the field at Indianapolis, the resurgence – and tragic eclipse – of Mercedes' racing activities, and the end of the domination of motor racing by front-engined cars. Things would never be the same.

▼ **AMAZING
MASERATI**

The archetypal
racing car of the
1950s, the six-
cylinder 2.5-litre
Maserati 250F
was built in three
series between
1954 and 1958.

# 1940-1960 Midget Racing

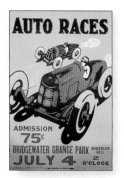

MIDGET
RACING POSTER

MIDGET RACING WAS born during the Depression in America in the 1930s to replace the depleted championship schedule. Midget cars are restricted to wheelbases of 168–193 cm (66–76 in) in length. However, the size of the cars does not diminish their performance, and speeds of up to 110 kph (70 mph) are possible. The races are held both on indoor and outdoor circuits varying in length from just 0.16 km (0.1 mile) to 1.6 km (1 mile). The formula has been a successful training ground for many oval track stars. Several Indianapolis winners, and world Formula One champion Mario Andretti, raced midgets. The sport reached a high point in the 1950s and, in 1955, the United States Auto Club formed a midget division which organizes up to 70 races a year.

### ▶ BRAIN VERSUS BRAWN

A rail-frame speedster powered by the reliable flathead Ford V8-60 engine leads against a tube-frame Kurtis "Offy" midget in a close race at Middletown, New York, in 1948. Although the Offy engine was technically superior, Fords still won races, often with the added advantage of a shot of nitromethane, referred to as "pop", in the fuel tank.

### ▼ RAIL-FRAME SPECIAL

Aaron Woodward's 1947 "Jimmy James Special" is one of around a thousand midgets manufactured by Frank Kurtis. The protective fender rails enabled it to be push-started

Fender rails

Transverse suspension

Ford chassis rails

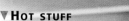

### ▶ POWER SLIDING

Five midgets demonstrate dirt-track cornering techniques at Gilmore Stadium, California. The track was named after oilman Earl Gilmore who had promoted the development of the Offy midget engine to replace the many unreliable homemade "junkyard" midget engines.

### ▼ HOT STUFF

Vic Sloan is pictured here in 1948 at the wheel of his classic rail-frame midget. With the addition of special light-alloy cylinder heads and dual Stromberg carburettors, the car's Ford V8-60 engine performed well. However, its liability to overheat earned it the nickname of "tea-kettle".

### FORD AT HEART

Hundreds of midgets, like this one, were built by amateur woodshed mechanics using Ford passenger car chassis parts.

### IT HAPPENED IN SUN VALLEY

Jimmy Ludlington won the Sun Valley Midget Speedway Race at Anderson, Indiana, in July 1948 with this Offy-powered midget. Early midgets had cut-down Model A Ford transmissions, giving two forward speeds. These were later abandoned in favour of simple one-speed dog-clutch transmission.

Exposed exhaust pipe

Carburettor bulge

### ADAPTABLE ENGINE

Another variant on the classic Ford V8-60 theme, Roy Duckworth's rail-frame midget dates from 1949. Although Ford and Offy engines were the favourite engines for these racers, some were modified to use Indian, Harley-Davidson or JAP motorbike engines, or even Elto four-cylinder two-stroke outboard motors.

### MISSIONARY ZEAL

These Ford V8-60-powered midgets were part of a team of American midget racers that came to Britain in the spring of 1948 in an attempt to popularize the sport. Over 60,000 English motor sport enthusiasts turned out to see them.

Radius rods to locate axle

### INDOOR FIREWORKS

This 1949 indoor contest in the Kingsbridge Armory, New York features Joe Barzola in an early tube-frame Kurtis, with Tony Bonadies on his right. Frank Kurtis built the chassis for his cars out of chrome-molybdenum tubing, and a Kurtis midget cost less than $2,800.

### SIX-CYLINDER SPECIAL

Good use was made of Ford parts in creating this "Knudsen Special". Its six-cylinder power unit featured a special Knudsen head with a three-carburettor manifold and overhead valve conversion.

69

# 1940-1960 Kurtis-Offenhauser

THE IMMEDIATE POSTWAR years saw a host of bright ideas at Indianapolis. The impetus came from southern California, where numerous specialist builders took the typical "Offy"-powered dirt-track car and refined it for the paved oval. Independently of Europe, they developed tubular chassis frames, fuel injection, disc braking and magnesium wheels, tubular shock absorbers, and torsion-bar independent suspension. Frank Kurtis was chief among the Californian racing-car builders. In the 1930s he realized that offsetting the engine gave a racer a distinct balance advantage on an oval track. Between 1950 and 1964, every Indianapolis 500 winner was either built by Kurtis or influenced by his designs.

### ▲ RAIN STOPPED PLAY

Johnnie Parsons drove this Kurtis-Offy to victory in the 1950 Indianapolis 500. The weather played a key role in his win because the race was halted after 138 laps, due to rain, thwarting the race strategy of rivals who were hanging back for a late assault.

*Handbrake*

*Gear lever*

*Instrument panel*

### ◄ WELL FINISHED

With its padded steering-wheel boss and neat layout, the Kurtis-Offy dashboard reflects its builder's roots in the Californian custom car business.

*Fuel filler*

*High-level exhaust*

*Padded steering wheel boss*

*Radius arm*

*Knock-off hubcap*

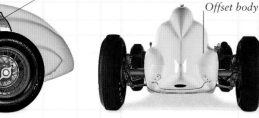

*Air intake*

**FRONT VIEW**

*Carburettor intake cover*

*Hand pump*

*Duplicated steering linkage*

**SIDE VIEW**

*Offset body*

**REAR VIEW**

## ▶ BIASED VIEW

Frank Kurtis was the first to devise the offset layout for oval-track racers. Moving the weight of the engine over towards the side of the racer that is nearer the inside of the track gives the car a better balance.

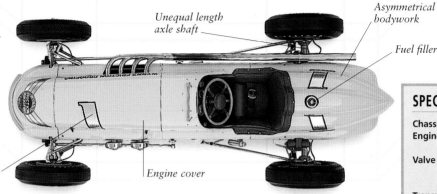

*Unequal length axle shaft*

*Asymmetrical bodywork*

*Fuel filler*

*Damascened racing number*

*Engine cover*

**TOP VIEW**

## ▼ CLASSIC DESIGN

The Kurtis-Offenhauser was a conventional tubular-framed dirt-track car, although the use of independent front suspension was an advanced feature. Early Kurtis-Offys had De Dion rear axles, but the car which Johnnie Parsons drove in the 1950 Indianapolis 500 had fully independent rear suspension controlled by torsion bars.

### SPECIFICATION

| | |
|---|---|
| **Chassis** | tubular spaceframe |
| **Engine** | Offy 4.5-litre four-cylinder |
| **Valve type** | two inlet, two exhaust; two overhead camshafts |
| **Transmission** | two-speed |
| **Power output** | 325 bhp |
| **Weight** | 725 kg (1,600 lb) |
| **Suspension** | torsion bar (front) torsion bar (rear) |
| **Top speed** | approx. 240 kph (approx.150 mph) |
| **Fuel** | aviation fuel (Avgas) |

*Sponsor's name*

*Eye-catching colour scheme*

*Firestone Deluxe Champion racing tyres*

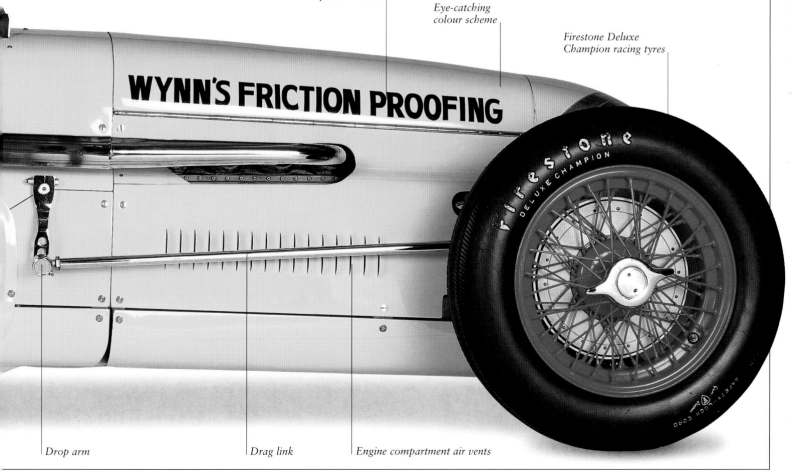

*Drop arm*

*Drag link*

*Engine compartment air vents*

# 1940-1960 The Argentine Grand Prix

*JUAN FANGIO'S AUTOBIOGRAPHY*

RACING IN ARGENTINA began in the early 1950s when the "17 de Octubre" circuit at Buenos Aires was first constructed. Argentina was the home of two of the greatest racing drivers of the 1950s, Juan Manuel Fangio and Froilan Gonzales. The country's president, Juan Peron, promoted the circuit to enhance the national prestige that the two drivers created. Maseratis and Ferraris dominated the races, with the two Argentine drivers taking many victories. The Argentine Grand Prix stopped in 1961, had a brief revival in the 1970s, then returned to a refurbished Buenos Aires circuit in 1995.

## ▲ DAMPENED ARDOUR

Froilan Gonzalez' first race for Ferrari was the 1954 Argentine Grand Prix. Although his new Type 625 2.5-litre Ferrari was faster than the rival Maseratis, its roadholding was inferior, and, after a tropical storm lashed the track, he could only manage to finish third.

## ▶ MASERATI TRIUMPH

During the 1950s, the Argentine Grand Prix opened the Formula One season. The 1957 race was a Maserati triumph, with Juan Fangio in his 250F leading his team-mates Jean Behra, Carlos Menditeguy, and Harry Schell to take the first four places.

## ▲ SUPERCHARGED MASERATI

Cars line up on the starting grid for the 1949 International Grand Prix of Juan Peron on the Palermo circuit, Buenos Aires. The race was won by Alberto Ascari's supercharged 260-hp 4CLT Maserati.

## ◀ WITH FLYING COLOURS

Painted in the distinctive blue and yellow livery of the Argentine Racing Club, the 1949 2-litre Ferrari 125/166 "America" was originally raced by Froilan Gonzalez and Juan Fangio in the Argentine series.

## ◀ HISTORIC MOMENT

Stirling Moss, driving this Cooper-Climax, won the first-ever world championship victory for a rear-engined car in 1958.

### ▶ VERSATILE WINNER

Alberto Ascari won the 1950 Argentine Grand Prix at the Mar del Plata circuit in this supercharged V12 1.5-litre Ferrari. Ascari also won the previous year's race driving a supercharged 4CLT/48 Maserati.

### ▲ NON-FINISHER

This is one of three 2.5-litre twin-cam six-cylinder Type 16 Gordinis that ran in the 1954 and 1955 Argentine Grands Prix, though not one of them finished. These French racers started life in 1952 with 2-litre power units.

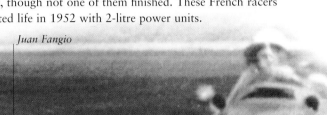

*Juan Fangio*

### ▲ PORSCHE PROTOTYPE

Ferdinand Porsche's first postwar Grand Prix car – the four-wheel drive 1949 Type 360 – was powered by a 1.5-litre flat-12 engine. When it ran in Argentina it was known as an "Autoar".

### 17 DE OCTUBRE

Until 1952, the Argentine Grand Prix had been held on closed-off public roads. President Peron then inaugurated the new "17 de Octubre" circuit, intended to put Argentina on the international motor-racing map. Slippery when wet, and plagued by appalling crowd control, the Buenos Aires autodrome was taken off the Formula One calendar after 1960. In 1971 international racing returned to Buenos Aires for ten years, then was revived again in 1995.

START/FINISH

### ▶ CHANCE FOR LANCIA

The Lancia D50 made its debut in the 1955 Argentine Grand Prix. Its 2.5-litre V8 power unit formed part of the front chassis structure, and outrigger fuel tanks gave optimum weight distribution. After the Lancia company's failure that year the project was handed over to Ferrari.

*Outrigger fuel tank*

# 1940-1960 The Maserati Marque

ITALY'S MASERATI brothers were famed tuners and racing mechanics long before they built their first car, which won its class in the 1926 Targa Florio. After the death of company founder Alfieri Maserati in 1932, his three remaining brothers carried on building highly successful racing and sports cars for both professional and amateur racing drivers. In its later years the company was backed by the wealthy Orsi family, who took over the business in 1947. Production was always small, but the tally of victories was immense.

◄ **SINGLE-SEAT LEGEND**

The fame of the Maserati 6CM-1500 far outstripped its modest production run. Just eleven of the original monoposto Tipo 6CM model were built between 1936 and 1939. The car was powered by a supercharged 1500cc twin-cam straight-six engine. The Tipo 6CM proved its mettle by beating the works ERA team at the Nürburgring in 1936.

▶ **INDY WINNER**

The 1938 Tipo 8CTF was originally built for the new 3-litre Grand Prix formula. The car had no Grand Prix success, but managed to win the 1939 Indianapolis 500.

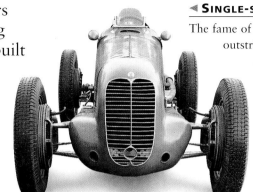

*Aeroscreen*

▼ **POPULAR PRIVATEER**

Maserati's first purpose-built single-seater, the Tipo 8CM, made its debut at the 1933 Tunis Grand Prix. With a 3-litre straight-eight engine, it had a top speed of 230 kph (144 mph) and was popular with private teams.

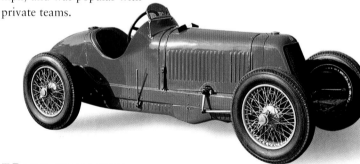

▼ **RACER IN DISGUISE**

This 1934 Tipo 6C/34 Maserati is a Grand Prix car, one of a series of six built between 1934 and 1935. As a 3.3-litre single-seater, the Tipo C/34 was successfully raced by Tazio Nuvolari; this one-off two-seater, fitted with a 3.7-litre power unit, ran in the 1935 Mille Miglia.

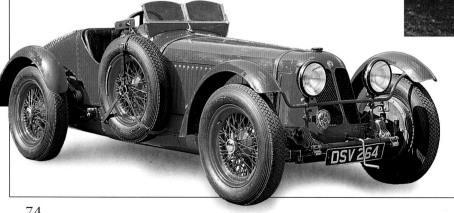

▲ **TUBULAR CHASSIS**

Derived from the prewar 4CL, the 4CLT (the T stands for "Tubolare", tubular chassis) made its debut at Reims in 1947 and was uprated the following year to become the 4CLT/48, which won many international events. Power came from a supercharged four-cylinder engine developing a remarkable 260 bhp, which gave this handsome racer a top speed of over 260 kph (155 mph).

## ▲ GRAND-PRIX WINNER

Built as a 2-litre Formula Two car from 1951, and later uprated to take a 2.5-litre Formula One power unit for 1954, the six-cylinder Tipo A6CGM is seen here in the masterly hands of Juan Manuel Fangio in the 1953 Swiss Grand Prix. Fangio won the 1953 Italian and Modena Grands Prix in this Maserati.

## ▼ ELEGANT COUPÉ

Featuring GT coupé bodywork by Pininfarina, the A6GCS coupé ran in the 1954 Circuit of Sicily road race. Initially launched in 1947 as an open-wheeled single-seater, the A6GCS appeared in a second series in 1953 with enveloping bodywork. The team of three works-entered cars ran in the Mille Miglia, winning the 2-litre class.

## ▼ BEAUTIFUL MACHINE

Perhaps the most beautiful postwar single-seat racer, the 2.5-litre Maserati 250F, was a major force in Grand Prix racing between 1954 and 1957. Here, drivers Piero Taruffi (no. 8) and Jean Behra (no. 4) prepare their 250F Maseratis for the 1956 French Grand Prix at Reims.

*19-inch (48-cm) knock-off wire wheel*

*Hole for starting handle*

*Ventilated drum brake*

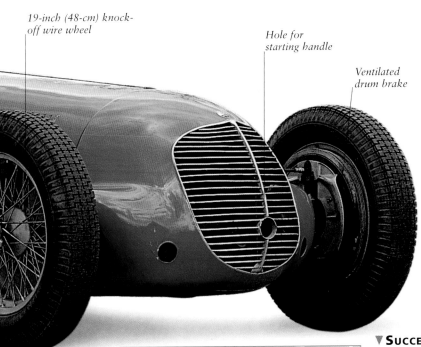

### RACING HIGHLIGHTS

**1926** Alfieri Maserati drives the first Maserati, the Tipo 26, to first place in the Targa Florio.

**1929** A 4-litre V16 Tipo V4 achieves the fastest speed yet set by a racing car, 246.1 kph (152.9 mph) at Cremona.

**1933** Tazio Nuvolari's Tipo 8CM wins the Belgian Grand Prix.

**1939** Wilbur Shaw's Tipo 8CTF wins the Indy 500.

**1957** Juan Fangio wins the world championship with his Maserati 250F.

## ▼ SUCCESSFUL SPORTS-RACER

The Tipo 300S was driven to victory by Stirling Moss and Jean Behra in the 1,000-km (625-mile) Nürburgring race of May 1956. This 3-litre model had a top speed of 290 kph (175 mph). The Tipo 300S was built from 1955 to 1958, and many were exported to the United States.

*Rear stabilizing fin*

## ◄ BIG BRUTE

The "Eldorado Special" was driven by Stirling Moss in the 1958 "Race of Two Worlds" between American and European cars at Monza. However, its 4.2-litre engine was too powerful for the chassis and brakes, and the car was withdrawn from the race after crashing.

# 1940-1960 Jaguar C-Type

FOR MANY people, the Jaguar C-Type epitomizes the true spirit of Le Mans – a practical sports-racing car that can be driven to the circuit, compete in the race, win, and be driven home again. To that already remarkable combination, the C-Type added a feline grace that has rarely been equalled. William Lyons, Jaguar's founder, was a fine stylist himself, but he left the shaping of the C-Type to master aerodynamicist Malcolm Sayer. Lyons insisted that the car, which was officially known as the XK120-C (C stands for "competition"), should have a family resemblance to the production XK120 sports car, but beneath its bodywork the C-Type concealed a rigid tubular frame. True to its purpose, the C-Type gave Jaguar its first Le Mans victory.

### ▲ WINNING FORMULA

Built to win at Le Mans, the C-type succeeded brilliantly, with victory in the 1951 race at a record speed. It also won races on both sides of the Atlantic, including the 360-km (224-mile) 1952 Sports Car Grand Prix at Reims, where it was driven to victory by Stirling Moss.

### ◄ RACING IN MIND

Laid out with racing in mind, the dashboard of the C-Type Jaguar concentrates all the essential information within the driver's line of vision.

### ▼ SHAPED IN THE WIND TUNNEL

Aerodynamicist Malcolm Sayer had worked for the Bristol Aeroplane Company, and the XK120-C was his very first design after moving to Jaguar. The car is lighter and more streamlined than the road-going XK120, but it retains the Jaguar "family resemblance", particularly in the swooping wing contours.

Quick-release fuel filler cap

Door for driver only – no passenger door

Aeroscreen

Steering wheel on telescopic column

Rear sub-frame

Knock-off wire wheel with light-alloy rim

High sill over tubular spaceframe

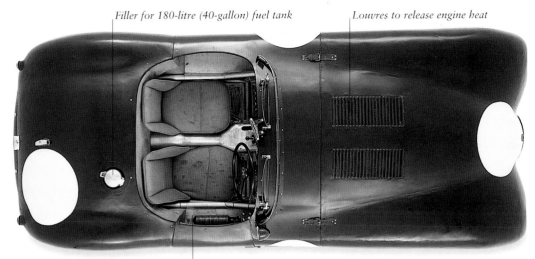

Filler for 180-litre (40-gallon) fuel tank

Louvres to release engine heat

Sill used to hold tools and plugs

TOP VIEW

## SPECIFICATION

| | |
|---|---|
| Chassis | tubular spaceframe |
| Engine | 3.4-litre in-line six cylinder |
| Valve type | one inlet, one exhaust; two overhead camshafts |
| Transmission | four-speed and reverse |
| Power output | 200 bhp |
| Weight | 1,015 kg (2,240 lb) |
| Suspension | independent torsion bar and wishbone (front) torsion bar and rigid axle (rear) |
| Top speed | 230 kph (144 mph) |
| Fuel | petrol |

Full-width Perspex windscreen

Stop light

Panel covering spare wheel

PUR 120

PUR 120

FRONT VIEW

Air intake maintains "family" look

REAR VIEW

Cross-ply road racing tyre

### ◄ FIT FOR THE PURPOSE

Just 54 C-Type Jaguars were built from 1951 to 1953, their purposeful lines placing them among the most handsome sports cars of all time. Because the car was designed for sports-racing, only a driver's door was provided: the passenger had to climb in over the side of the car, avoiding the hot exhaust pipe.

Roundel for racing number

Front-hinged bonnet for maximum accessibility

Faired-in headlamps

Bonnet release handle

Knock-off hubcap

## 1940-1960 The British Grand Prix

THE 1950s WAS a golden decade of motor racing in Britain. The British Racing Motors (BRM) project promised much, although in fact achieved very little, but the short-lived Vanwall company had some success. British racing drivers such as Stirling Moss and Mike Hawthorn were world class. After the dismal years of postwar austerity, motor sport was burgeoning. Several World War II airfields were adapted to create race circuits, such as Silverstone and Goodwood, while the track at Aintree was laid out alongside the horse-racing course.

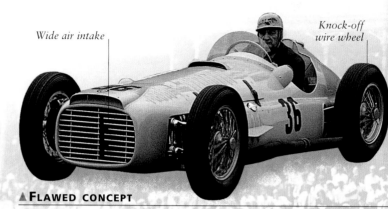

Wide air intake

Knock-off wire wheel

### ▲ FLAWED CONCEPT

Complex and unreliable, the 1.5-litre centrifugally supercharged V16 BRM was conceived by designer Raymond Mays as the flagship of Britain's postwar motor racing effort. It could develop 485 bhp, but came only fifth and seventh in the 1951 British Grand Prix championship.

### ▲ GOODWOOD WINNER

Mike Hawthorn is pictured here in the 4.5-litre Ferrari-based Thin Wall Special which won both Formula Libre events at the 1953 Goodwood International Meeting. Goodwood, an airfield circuit in Sussex, was the home of the British Automobile Racing Club.

Jean Behra

### ▼ FLYING FERRARI

Frenchman Maurice Trintignant is seen here driving a Ferrari in the 1955 British Grand Prix at Aintree. Overheating caused him to withdraw the car on the 59th lap.

Large brake drum

### ▲ ANCIENT AND MODERN

The 1950 two-stage supercharged 1.5-litre Grand Prix Alta never lived up to its promise. Here, Joe Kelly's Alta, on the left, dices with Brian Shawe-Taylor's prewar ERA in the 1951 British Grand Prix at Silverstone. The ERA finished eighth with the Alta nine laps behind in last place.

Straight-through exhaust

Wraparound
windscreen

High-level
exhaust

## ▲ VICTORIOUS V12

The Argentinian Froilan Gonzales came to Silverstone with this 4.5-litre V12 Ferrari for the 1951 British Grand Prix. His winning drive broke a long run of Alfa Romeo victories.

## ▲ FINAL SEASON

The four-cylinder twin-cam Vanwall won the World Championship in 1958. Its 2.5-litre engine produced a top speed of 280 kph (175 mph). The Vanwall team was disbanded at the end of 1958 because of the ill health of the team's backer, Tony Vandervell.

Juan Manuel Fangio

Stirling Moss

## ▼ MERCEDES WIN

Aintree was the venue for the exciting 1955 British Grand Prix in which Stirling Moss in a straight-eight W196 Mercedes achieved his first Grand Prix win, beating Juan Fangio, also in a Mercedes, by the length of his car.

## ▼ ARGENTINE DREAM

A familiar sight in the early 1950s was that of the brilliant Argentinian driver Juan Manuel Fangio at the wheel of his Alfa Romeo 158, seen here in the 1951 British Grand Prix at Silverstone.

# 1940-1960 Mercedes W196

BONNET
BADGE

IN RESPONSE to the new 2.5-litre formula announced for 1954, Mercedes returned to Formula One racing for the first time since World War II. The new W196 racer drew on the company's experience with the 300SL sports car and used a spaceframe composed of small-diameter tubes. Its straight-eight 2.5-litre engine was canted over to the right to reduce height and keep the centre of gravity low, and was equipped with direct fuel injection. Among the other ingenious features of this design were turbocooled inboard brakes front and rear to keep unsprung weight to a minimum. The W196 raced in both fully streamlined and open-wheeled configurations, depending on the type of circuit on which it was competing.

## ▲ ASTOUNDING RECORD

Juan Manuel Fangio is seen here driving a Mercedes W196 in the Argentine Grand Prix in 1955, when he won the world championship. The W196 had an astounding racing record, winning the very first event for which it was entered, the 1954 French Grand Prix. Fangio came first, followed by team-mate Karl Kling.

## ▼ DISTINCTIVE PROFILE

The spaceframe of the W196 enables a very low driving position and gives the car a most distinctive profile, quite unlike any of its Formula One rivals. Because the car has inboard brakes, the remote electric starter has to be inserted through a hole in the car's tail.

*Fuel filler flap*

*Removable steering wheel*

*Air escape duct*

*Oil tank filler flap*

*Three-eared knock-off wheel nut*

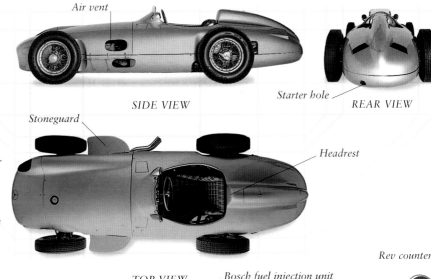

FRONT VIEW

Air intake

Air vent

SIDE VIEW

Starter hole

REAR VIEW

Stoneguard

Headrest

TOP VIEW

## ▶ FIT FOR THE PURPOSE

This open-wheeled version of the W196 proved more practical for Grands Prix than the full-width streamlined body. Enclosing the wheels made it very difficult for drivers to place the car accurately on the racetrack.

## ▶ NO SPRINGS

The valves of the low-profile straight-eight W196 engine are desmodromic – they are positively opened and closed without the use of springs.

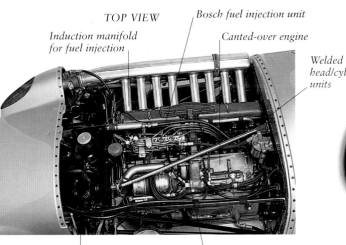

Induction manifold for fuel injection

Bosch fuel injection unit

Canted-over engine

Welded head/cylinder units

Steering box

Steering column

### SPECIFICATION

| | |
|---|---|
| Chassis | tubular spaceframe |
| Engine | 2.5-litre straight-eight |
| Valve type | one inlet, one exhaust; desmodromic |
| Transmission | five-speed |
| Power output | 300 bhp |
| Weight | 640 kg (1,410 lb) |
| Suspension | torsion bar swing-axle (rear); torsion bar (front) |
| Top speed | 280 kph (175 mph) |
| Fuel | Benzol/methyl alcohol/petrol mix |

Oil gauge

Removable steering wheel

Rev counter

Brake pedal

Gear lever

## ▲ SIMPLE LAYOUT

Although the W196 has more comfortable seating than the average Grand Prix car of its day, its dashboard is clinical in its simplicity, with the minimum of instrumentation.

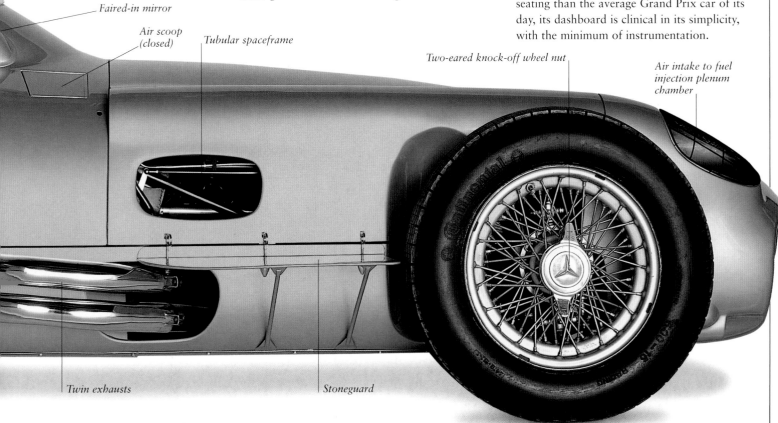

Aeroscreen

Faired-in mirror

Air scoop (closed)

Tubular spaceframe

Two-eared knock-off wheel nut

Air intake to fuel injection plenum chamber

Twin exhausts

Stoneguard

# 1940-1960 The Ferrari Marque

THE AUTOCRATIC ENZO Ferrari established the Scuderia Ferrari racing team to organize the racing interests of the Alfa Romeo company in 1929. After leaving Alfa Romeo, Enzo Ferrari built two 8-cylinder sports cars in 1939, and became a manufacturer under his own name in 1947, when he unveiled his new V12 sports car. From then on the company was primarily a racing-car manufacturer, with road cars built to finance Ferrari's racing efforts. Ferrari's record of Grand Prix success is unrivalled, and they have taken the Formula One constructors' championship on eight occasions.

### ▲ WAR OF ATTRITION

There were three major participants in the 1954 Italian Grand Prix. Alberto Ascari's Ferrari (centre) was a stopgap design, with a Type 553 engine in a 625 chassis, and it dominated the race until the engine burst. The ensuing battle between the Mercedes (left) driven by Juan Fangio and the Maserati of Stirling Moss was won by Fangio.

### ▲ FERRARI WINS IN JAPAN

Michael Schumacher won the 1997 Japanese Grand Prix at Suzuka in this Ferrari F310B with a Type 046 V10 engine. His chief rival Jacques Villeneuve was disqualified. However, Villeneuve then won the last race of the season and became the champion.

*Low bonnet line*

*Pannier fuel tank*

### ▲ TARGA WINNER

This 166 Ferrari Sport was hastily cobbled together for Prince Igor Troubetskoi's Gruppo Inter motor racing organization in the late 1940s. It was fitted with an early Ferrari 1500cc V12 engine uprated to 2 litres. It proved an effective sports racer, and Troubetskoi drove it to victory in the sports class of the 1948 Targa Florio.

### RACING HIGHLIGHTS

| | |
|---|---|
| 1947 | First victory for the new Ferrari 166GP in the Garda races. |
| 1949 | A Ferrari 166 Barchetta wins the first postwar Le Mans 24-hour race. |
| 1951 | Froilan Gonzalez secures Ferrari's first victory at Silverstone in a 4.5-litre 375. |
| 1952 | Alberto Ascari wins Ferrari's first world championship in a Type 500. |
| 1956 | A brilliant year for Ferrari, thanks to the Lancia-Ferrari D50 Grand Prix car, which gives Juan Fangio the world championship. |
| 1961 | The first of eight constructors' championships for Ferrari (the others are 1964, '75, '76, '77, '79, '82 and '83). |
| 1962 | A 4-litre Testa Rossa wins the last major sports car victory for a front-engined Ferrari at Le Mans. |
| 1997 | By the end of the season, Ferrari have gained 113 Grand Prix wins overall. |

### ▲ IN THE COCKPIT

This driver's-eye view of the Troubetskoi Ferrari 166 shows its no-nonsense instrument panel. A development of this car, the 166 MM Barchetta, won a famous victory in the first postwar Le Mans race in 1949.

## ▲ SPECIAL SPORTSTER

This lovely Fantuzzi-bodied Ferrari Dino 196S resembles the classic V12 Testa Rossa sports-racer but is fitted with a 2.4-litre V6 "Dino 246" engine. Driven in 1960 by the Rodriguez brothers at Sebring, and in the Targa Florio, it was later raced by Luigi Chinetti's NART team.

## ▶ RACING DOWN UNDER

This car, built for New Zealand driver Chris Amon to race in the 1967 Tasman Series, originally used a 65-degree V6 Dino power unit. This engine was then replaced by the 2.4-litre, 18 valve 246 V6 power unit, mounted here in its brand-new "Aero" monocoque chassis.

*2.4 litre, 18 valve V6 engine*

*High-level exhaust pipe*

*Protective shield for driver's elbow*

*Rear tank filler cap*

## ▲ ROCKET-LIKE ACCELERATION

Ferrari's first monocoque Grand Prix car, the 312B3, appeared in 1973, and was completely revised during the winter of 1973–74. Its flat-12 engine developed a claimed 490 bhp and produced a top speed comfortably in excess of 250 kph (160 mph). Niki Lauda drove the car to two Grands Prix victories during the 1974 season.

## ▲ SUPERSHARK

An improved version of the 2-litre four-cylinder Tipo 553 "Squalo" ("shark"), the Tipo 555 "Supersqualo" appeared in 1955. It had a completely new chassis frame and a tubular superstructure carrying rear suspension, body, and fuel tanks.

## ▼ TURBOCHARGED RACER

In 1980, Ferrari introduced its turbocharged V6 engine; this 1.5-litre turbocharged 126C2B was built in 1982 and updated to 1983 specification for the first races of the new season. Driven by Patrick Tambay, this car finished fifth in the 1983 Brazilian Grand Prix.

## ▲ LACK OF SPEED

Michele Alboreto drove this Ferrari 126C4 in the 1984 British Grand Prix at Brands Hatch, but the car lacked speed, in spite of its claimed 660 bhp power output. The car had a revised radiator configuration intended to improve aerodynamics. Alboreto finished fifth, despite being balked by Andrea de Cesaris's Ligier.

# 1940-1960 Racing at Indianapolis

*INDY 500 PROGRAMME*

THE INDIANAPOLIS, or "Indy", 500 was instituted in the United States in 1911 and attracts huge crowds every Memorial Day holiday weekend. However, by the end of World War II, its future was in doubt. Abandoned and choked with weeds, the brick-surfaced race-track seemed beyond repair. Local entrepreneur Tony Hulman had the foresight to revive the crumbling Indianapolis track and ushered in a golden era for all American racers. The 1950s races were dominated by Kurtis-built cars powered by the long-established "Offy" engine. In 1955, Hulman was instrumental in setting up the United States Auto Club to run the nation's motor sport.

## ▲ HOT-STUFF WINNER

Bill Vukovich holds the massive Borg-Warner Trophy after winning the 1953 Indianapolis 500 in his Offy-powered Fuel Injection Special. The Californian Vukovich led for 195 of the 200 laps after starting from pole position. Towering behind the car is the Pagoda stand, a feature of the improved Indianapolis circuit.

## ▼ DIESEL REVOLUTION

This 1950 supercharged 6.6-litre diesel, with a production Cummins engine in a Kurtis speedway chassis, raced in that year's Indy 500. As early as 1931 a Cummins diesel racer was entered at Indianapolis, finishing 13th.

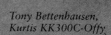

*Tony Bettenhausen, Kurtis KK300C-Offy*

## INDIANAPOLIS

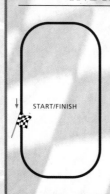

START/FINISH

Indianapolis is basically a rectangle with curved corners. The track has a total lap distance of 4 km (2.5 miles) made up of two 1-km (0.625-mile) straights and two 0.2-km (0.125-mile) straights linked by four 0.4-km (0.25-mile) banked turns. After the 1955 race, the "brickyard" was resurfaced with asphalt. However, for reasons of tradition, a stretch of bricks was preserved on the front straight.

## ▶ TRAGIC RACE

The last year that a Kurtis won Indianapolis was 1955, when the laydown KK500C driven by Bob Sweikert came through from 14th position on the grid. The race was interrupted by a multi-car crash on lap 57 in which driver Bill Vukovich, who had won the race twice before, was killed.

*Jack McGrath, Kurtis KK2000C-Offy*

## ▼ FAST BUT THIRSTY

The fastest Indianapolis car of its day was the front-wheel drive Novi Governor Special, based on a Kurtis chassis and powered by a supercharged quad-cam 3-litre V8. The Novi had a high fuel consumption and lost to the less powerful Blue Crown Specials.

### ▲ POPULAR CHOICE

Marshall Teague entered this Kurtis K4000 Fullerton Special for the 1954 Indianapolis 500 but failed to qualify. The K4000 was the standard car for Kurtis customers and was capable of racing anywhere from dirt tracks to Indianapolis.

### ▶ TWO-TIMES VICTOR

George Salih's Belond Special laydown roadster, driven here by Jimmy Bryan, heads for its second Indianapolis win in 1958. In 1957 Salih had convinced Offenhauser designer Leo Goossen to create a new version of the Offy four-cylinder engine that could be laid almost horizontal.

*Fred Agabashian,
Kurtis KK500C-Offy*

*Jerry Hoyt,
Stevens-Offy*

### ▲ ON THE TURN

Led by Walt Faulkner's Grant Piston Ring Special, contestants enter the first turn in the 1950 Indy 500. The race was won by Johnnie Parsons in a Wynn's Friction Special Kurtis-Offy.

### ▲ LONG LINEAGE

This Belond Equa Flow Exhaust Special Kurtis Kraft car was driven by Johnnie Parsons at Indianapolis in 1954. Every car in the race was Offy powered, nearly all with the 4.4-litre version of the twin-cam engine that traced its roots back to the 1912 French Grand Prix Peugeot.

*Ansted Rotary Special*

*Lindsey Hopkins Special*

*John Zink Special*

### ▶ FRONT ROW OF THE GRID

The John Zink Special, built by A.J. Watson and driven by Pat Flaherty, won the 1956 Indy 500 and broke the Kurtis stranglehold. The other cars are Jim Rathman's Lindsey Hopkins Special and Pat O'Connor's Ansted Rotary Special.

# THE INFLUENCE OF AMERICA

PERHAPS THE MOST dramatic period of change in motor-racing history – the decade of the 1960s – was dominated by bold new rear-engined designs and the emergence of sponsorship as a major force in the financing of Formula One. It had, of course, long been a feature of the Indianapolis scene, but the replacement of national racing colours by sponsors' livery created shockwaves around the Grand Prix circuits of the world. No less surprising was the rapid eclipse of the front-engined layout. Rear engines were not a new feature, but they had always been regarded as an exception to the norm. The turning point came with Cooper's victory in the 1959 world championship. While there had not been a rear-engined world championship winner prior to 1959, the impact of Cooper's win meant that there would never be a front-engined winner again. Only Ferrari attempted to resist change; but the Italian giant lasted a season before succumbing to the rear-engined trend, after which it won the world championship.

◄ **CHANGING TIMES**

The designer of this poster for the Monaco Grand Prix was behind the times, because the picture shows a front-engined racer which was obsolete by 1960.

▼ **TRUE COLOURS**

The Ford-Cosworth DFV-powered Lotus 49 in sponsorship livery represents an enduring image of motor racing during the 1960s.

# 1960-1970 The Italian Grand Prix

MONZA GRAND PRIX POSTER

THE ORIGINAL MONZA Autodrome opened in a former royal park in 1922. The first banked track was demolished in 1939 and the road circuit was rebuilt nine years later. This circuit was then supplemented by a new banked speed bowl in 1955. Although the road circuit was revised at the same time, the uneven road surface of the speed bowl was considered to be dangerous by the drivers, which caused a mass boycott of the 1960 Italian Grand Prix. Monza was the scene of some of the most exciting races of the late 1960s, with Lotus and Matra cars fighting for supremacy.

*Flat-eight engine giving low profile*

*Wraparound windscreen*

## ▲ BIGGER BEETLE?

Despite Porsche's success in other areas of motor sport, it has been largely unproductive in Formula One. In 1962 Porsche unveiled the flat-eight Type 804, but it was already outclassed and its driver, Dan Gurney, failed to finish at Monza, complaining that the car handled like a Volkswagen Beetle.

## ▼ CLOSE FINISH FOR MATRA

Jackie Stewart's Matra-Ford leads the field into the Parabolica curve in the 1969 Italian Grand Prix. Stewart won by half a car's length from Jochen Rindt in the closest finish ever seen in a Grand Prix. Stewart's win gave him the world championship.

## ▼ PIPPED AT THE POST

Jack Brabham, driving this Repco-Brabham, looked like a certain winner of the 1967 Italian Grand Prix. He led as the cars went into the final bend only to be overtaken by John Surtees' Honda V12 on the way out.

### MONZA

START/FINISH

Monza has been the home of Italian motor racing since 1922, though the circuit has been updated several times. It hosted some of the most exciting races of the 1960s, including Jackie Stewart's famous 1969 win.

*Piers Courage's Brabham-Ford BT28*

*Jochen Rindt's Lotus-Ford 49B*

## ▲ OUT OF CONTENTION

Driving the lightweight H16 BRM, Jackie Stewart was never in the running for the 1967 Italian Grand Prix. He had to make an early pit stop to cure a sticking throttle, and engine problems put his car out in the 46th lap.

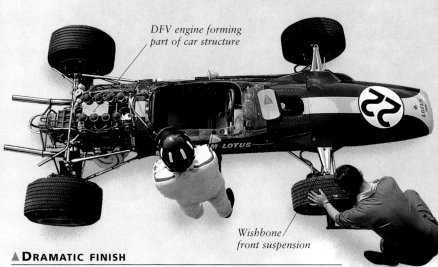

*DFV engine forming part of car structure*

*Wishbone front suspension*

## ▲ DRAMATIC FINISH

Graham Hill's Lotus-Ford looked set to win the 1967 Italian Grand Prix when its timing gear failed. Despite the loss of a lap due to a flat tyre, Jim Clark's sister car made up the lost ground and held the lead until the last lap, when he ran short of fuel.

*Aerofoil for stability*

## ▶ TAKING WING

For 1968 Ferrari carried out serious aerodynamic development of their racing cars. This 246 FL was built for the Tasman Series and fitted with a small aerofoil above the rear wheels to improve stability.

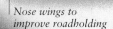

*Nose wings to improve roadholding*

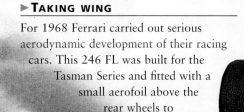

*Bruce McLaren's McLaren-Ford M7C*

*Jo Siffert's Lotus-Ford 49B*

*Jackie Stewart's Matra-Ford MS80*

# 1960-1970 The Monaco Grand Prix

*Carburettor trumpets*  
*Twin exhausts*

*MONACO RACE PROGRAMME*

WHEN THE FIRST championship Grand Prix was held at Monaco in 1950, the circuit had changed little since prewar days. Then a multiple pile-up on the very first lap of the race seemed to confirm its obsolescence, and no further championship races were held there for another five years.

However, by the 1960s the race had become the most glamorous fixture on the calendar. The Englishman Graham Hill was by far the most successful driver on this uniquely demanding circuit during the 1960s. He won the race five times, initially driving the 1.5-litre BRM, with his last two victories coming at the wheel of the 3-litre Lotus 49.

## ▲ BAD LUCK FOR MATRA

Jean-Pierre Beltoise gave Matra their first Formula One victory at a non-championship race at Cape Town in 1968, but his Matra V12 had less luck at Monaco. Beltoise damaged its front suspension by hitting the chicane on the eleventh lap and had to retire.

*Denny Hulme, McLaren-Ford*

*Jack Brabham, Repco-Brabham*

## ▲ FIGHTING BACK

Lorenzo Bandini had little luck driving this Ferrari in the 1964 Monaco Grand Prix. From seventh place on the starting grid he had reached fourth by lap 63, but gearbox trouble forced his car out of the race five laps later.

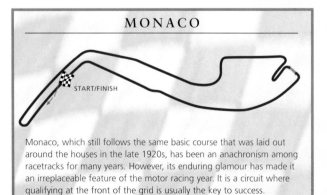

### MONACO

START/FINISH

Monaco, which still follows the same basic course that was laid out around the houses in the late 1920s, has been an anachronism among racetracks for many years. However, its enduring glamour has made it an irreplaceable feature of the motor racing year. It is a circuit where qualifying at the front of the grid is usually the key to success.

## ▲ SHOWING THE STRAIN

The strains imposed on competing cars by the tight Monaco circuit were shown in 1968 when John Surtees' Honda V12 experienced severe transmission problems in practice, despite recording the third-fastest time.

## ▼ HIGH CASUALTY RATE

The 1968 Monaco Grand Prix saw its famous chicane moved towards the Tabac corner and made sharper. This caught some drivers out, and only five of the 16 starters were still running at quarter-distance.

*Pedro Rodriguez, BRM*

*Jean-Pierre Beltoise, Matra V12*

## ▲ MASERATI BEATEN

Despite the advent of the 3-litre Formula One, the 1966 Monaco Grand Prix proved a victory for the old order. Jo Bonnier's V12 Cooper-Maserati was one of only two 3-litre cars to finish. Bonnier finished 25 laps behind the winner, Jackie Stewart in a 2-litre BRM.

*Rear-mounted V12 BRM engine*

*Laid-back driving position*

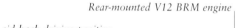

## ▲ BIG TROUBLE

Driving this Cooper-BRM, Italian driver Ludovico Scarfiotti had a difficult race at Monaco in 1968. He hit the chicane and blew a tyre, and his car's engine also had valve trouble. In spite of these difficulties, Scarfiotti managed to complete the race as one of only five finishers.

## ▲ CONSISTENT WINNER

Graham Hill took the second of three consecutive Monaco Grands Prix wins in 1964 with this BRM V8. However, he just missed out on the world championship that season when he was delayed by a collision with Lorenzo Bandini's Ferrari in the Mexican Grand Prix.

# 1960-1970 Indianapolis Lotus-Ford Type 29

THE MOST SIGNIFICANT racing combination of the postwar years was that of Lotus and Ford, which combined the iconoclastic genius of Colin Chapman with the big-corporation muscle of a major mass-producer. Lotus-Fords were already doing well on the racetracks of Europe when Colin Chapman was introduced to Indianapolis and realized that he could build a car capable of winning the Indianapolis 500. Ford, who had recently started a major competition programme, were cooperative. The result of the collaboration was the Lotus-Ford 29, which almost won Indianapolis on its first attempt in 1963. Two years later driver Jim Clark secured the victory that Chapman and Ford had hoped for.

### ▲ START OF SOMETHING BIG

Jim Clark in the Lotus 29 leads two rivals into a bend during the 1963 Indianapolis 500. Clark eventually finished in second place, although it was suggested that the winner, Parnelli Jones, should have been called into the pits for dropping oil on the track. Lotus's second place marked the demise of the old generation of front-engined Indy cars.

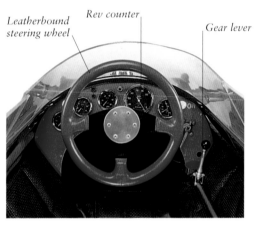

*Leatherbound steering wheel*  
*Rev counter*  
*Gear lever*

### ◀ COMPACT COCKPIT

The neat arrangement of the instruments on the horseshoe-shaped dashboard of the Lotus 29 reflects Chapman's training as an aircraft engineer.

### ▼ LUCKY FOR SOME

Based on the Lotus 25, the Lotus 29 is slightly longer and wider but follows the same aircraft-type monocoque construction principles. The car featured Chapman's favoured reclining driving position, something new at Indianapolis. It also defied an old Indy superstition that it was unlucky to run a green car at the Brickyard.

*Forward fuel tank*  
*Wraparound windscreen*  
*Nose section containing radiator and oil tank*  
*LOTUS F*  
*Centre-lock Dunlop racing wheels*  
*Wide sill holding fuel bag*

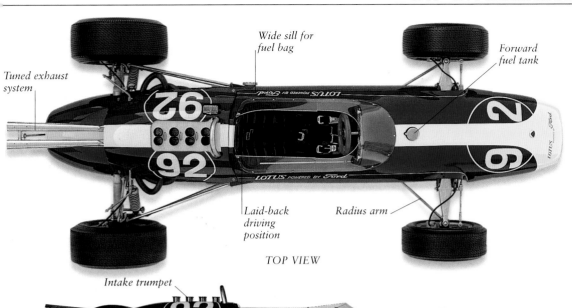

Tuned exhaust system

Wide sill for fuel bag

Forward fuel tank

Laid-back driving position

Radius arm

**TOP VIEW**

### SPECIFICATION

| | |
|---|---|
| Chassis | aluminium alloy monocoque |
| Engine | V8 |
| Valve type | overhead inlet push-rod overhead |
| Transmission | four-speed Colotti (only two speeds used at Indy) |
| Power output | 376 bhp |
| Weight | 590 kg (1,300 lb) |
| Suspension | coil and wishbone (front) coil and wishbone (rear) |
| Top speed | 240 kph (150 mph) |
| Fuel | petrol |

#### ▼ LEANING TO THE LEFT

Colin Chapman fitted the Lotus 29 with asymmetrical wishbone suspension to shift the body 6 cm (2.5 in) to the left, to obtain the optimum bias for the banked left-hand turns of the oval circuit.

Intake trumpet

**SIDE VIEW**

Wide rear tyre

Offset body

Short wishbone

Long wishbone

Narrow front tyre

**FRONT VIEW**

Air intake

**REAR VIEW**

Colotti gear box

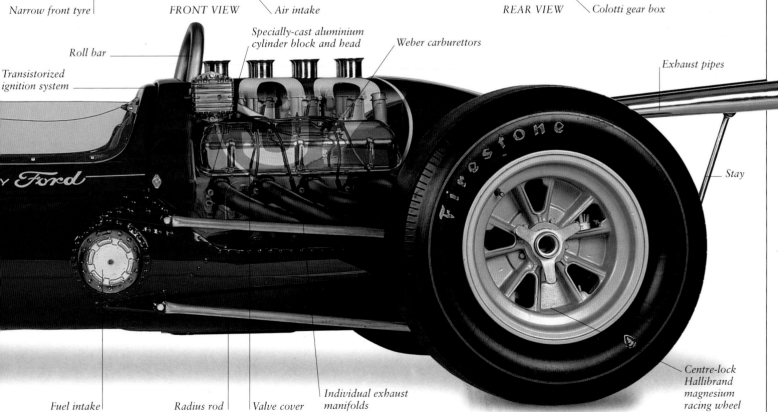

Roll bar

Specially-cast aluminium cylinder block and head

Weber carburettors

Exhaust pipes

Transistorized ignition system

Stay

Fuel intake

Radius rod

Valve cover

Individual exhaust manifolds

Centre-lock Hallibrand magnesium racing wheel

# 1960-1970 Racing at Le Mans

*LE MANS RACE PROGRAMME*

THE SARTHE CIRCUIT at Le Mans, France, is the venue for the most famous endurance race in motor sport. Originally held in 1923 as a test of the reliability and efficiency of production cars, the race takes place over a period of 24 hours, though the days when a standard sports car could win it are long gone. The 1960s saw a battle for supremacy between Ford and Ferrari. Frustrated in his bid to buy the Italian company, Ford's owner, Henry Ford II, resolved to defeat Ferrari on the race-track and made a huge investment in developing top-class sports cars to race at Le Mans.

*Doors open into roof*

*NACA duct (air intake)*

## ▲ DETROIT WINNERS

This 7-litre Ford Mk IV driven by the two-man team of McLaren and Donohue came fourth at Le Mans in 1967. The Ford company, of Detroit, USA, entered four Mk IVs and three Mk IIBs, all with 7-litre engines, together with three 4.7-litre GT40s. The Mk IV driven by Gurney and Foyt scored the first-ever all-American Le Mans win.

*Lamps set at regulation height*

*Air intake*

## ▲ FERRARI TRIUMPH

The 1964 race was the first to see a Ford entry, though the Ferrari driven by Guichet and Vaccarella won the Italian marque's eighth Le Mans. The traditional sprint across the track to jump into the cars had been a feature of the race since the very beginning in 1923.

## ▲ SNAKE CHARMER

Bolton and Sanderson drove this AC Cobra to seventh place at Le Mans in 1963, making it the highest-placed British car. Standard sports cars like this one, which could be raced by amateurs, were still a feature of the Le Mans entry list in the 1960s, despite the arrival of the big battalions.

## ▲ WIDE-RANGING ENTRY

A 2-litre Type 906 Porsche was driven by Poirot and Koch at Le Mans in 1967. Though the focus of the race was the continuing duel between Ford and Ferrari, Porsche fielded a wider range of cars in 1967 than other manufacturers, with entries in prototype, sports, and GT classes.

### LE MANS

The Le Mans circuit, which is part private track and part closed-off public roads, changed little between 1932 and 1967. The Ford Chicane was introduced in 1967 just before the grandstand area to slow the cars down in the interests of safety.

## ▲ CLASS WINNER

This little Alpine Renault A210 won the 1300cc class in 1966, driven by Grandsire and Cella. Success at Le Mans is not just a matter of being first across the line after 24 hours; the race has many classes, and victory in these is as highly prized as an outright win.

*Rear-mounted gas turbine*

## ▲ JET COUPÉ

The Rover company's long-term programme of gas-turbine car development saw this neat two-seater jet coupé entered at Le Mans in 1965. Driven by Graham Hill and Jackie Stewart, it was the first British car to finish.

## ◄ ITALIAN SUPERCAR

Barney and Noblet's 5.3-litre Iso Rivolta, which was entered by the Société Sonauto, leads a 2-litre Prototype Porsche around Arnage in the 1964 Le Mans race.

## ▲ ITALIAN RECOVERY

Following their resounding defeat in 1966, Ferrari entered their new 4-litre P4 for the 1967 Le Mans race. Though a 7-litre Ford Mk IV was still outright winner, this P4 driven by Scarfiotti and Parkes finished second and won the 5000cc class.

# 1960-1970 The Lotus Marque

LOTUS SEEMED INVINCIBLE in the 1960s and 1970s, consistently taking both the drivers' and manufacturers' championships. Spurred on by the energy of its founder, Colin Chapman, the company was a consistent innovator. It pioneered "active" suspension and "ground-effect" to suck the car on to the track for greater cornering power. Lotus often bent the rules of motor sport to breaking point, and the revolutionary twin-chassis design for the Lotus 88 caused such controversy that the car was banned from three Grands Prix in 1982. Chapman's background in aircraft engineering produced many imaginative ideas, but his designs had a sometimes well-founded reputation for fragility.

▲ **SPONSORSHIP DEAL**

The 1968 Gold Leaf Team Lotus 49B won the world championship for Graham Hill and the constructors' championship for its makers. It was also the first Formula One car to carry sponsors' livery.

*Faired-in front wheel*  *Cockpit cowling*  *Aerodynamic headrest*

▲ **SUCCESSFUL STREAMLINER**

The Lotus Eleven first appeared in 1956, with stressed-skin alloy streamlined bodywork designed by Frank Costin. The design was capable of taking a wide range of power units from 750cc up to 2.5 litres.

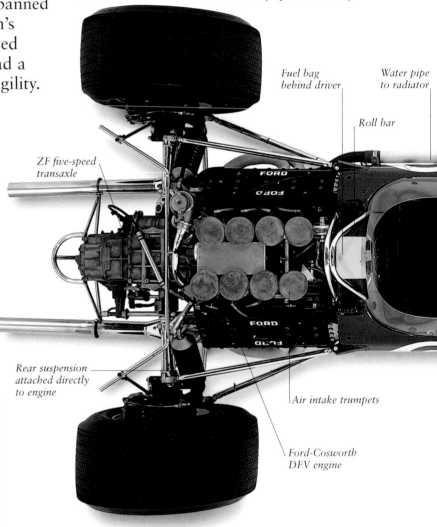

*Fuel bag behind driver*  *Water pipe to radiator*

*ZF five-speed transaxle*  *Roll bar*

*Rear suspension attached directly to engine*

*Air intake trumpets*

*Ford-Cosworth DFV engine*

▲ **HIGH SPEED GAS**

Always ready to try new ideas, Lotus built this Type 56B gas turbine Formula One car in 1971 and raced it in Gold Leaf Team Lotus colours in several Grands Prix. However, it only finished once, when Emerson Fittipaldi took eighth place in the Italian Grand Prix at Monza.

▲ **STORYBOOK WINNER**

The Formula One Lotus 49 was designed by Maurice Phillipe to take the new Ford-Cosworth DFV V8 engine, developed at Colin Chapman's instigation with £100,000 of Ford funding. The car, driven by Jim Clark, was a first-time winner in the 1967 Dutch Grand Prix.

*Aerodynamic suspension arm*

*Sidepod skirt seal*

*Roll bar*

## ▲ VERSATILE RACER

The 1960 Lotus Type 18 had a multitube chassis whose ingenious suspension enhanced stability. This versatile car was raced in various formulae with different engines.

## ▶ AERODYNAMIC WEDGE

The 1977 "John Player Special" III Lotus 78 had concealed inverted aerofoil sections hidden in the sidepods. These produced downthrust to give the car tremendous cornering power.

## ▶ BREAKING INDY MONOPOLY

Jim Clark's 4.2-litre Ford V8-powered Lotus 29 finished second in the Indianapolis 500 of 1963. The Lotus success broke the 40-year monopoly of cars powered by the Miller/Offenhauser twin-cam engine.

*Wishbone and strut suspension*

*Air intake to front radiator*

*Lateral fuel bag*

*Brake disc running in airstream*

*Suspension wishbone*

*Elbow cut-out*

*Kevlar bodywork*

*Pull-rod front suspension*

## ▶ TEAM RECORD-BREAKER

The 1986 Renault-powered 98T was the last John Player Special Lotus. This car, driven by Ayrton Senna, recorded the fastest-ever Lotus race speed of 346.24 kph (215.23 mph).

## RACING HIGHLIGHTS

| | |
|---|---|
| 1958 | The first Formula One race for Lotus – a Type 12 finishes sixth in the Monaco Grand Prix. |
| 1960 | Stirling Moss secures Lotus's first Formula One victory driving Rob Walker's Lotus 18 in the Monaco Grand Prix. |
| 1963 | Jim Clark wins the world drivers' championship in a Lotus 25. Lotus also win the manufacturers' championship. |
| 1965 | The second world championship double for Jim Clark and Lotus. Clark wins the Indianapolis 500 with a Lotus-Ford. |
| 1967 | The new Ford-Cosworth-engined Lotus 49 dominates Formula One racing from its first appearance. |
| 1968 | Graham Hill wins the world championship in the Lotus 49B. Lotus win the manufacturers' championship. |
| 1970 | A posthumous world championship for Jochen Rindt who is killed in practice at Monza in his Lotus 72. Lotus win the manufacturers' championship |
| 1972 | Emerson Fittipaldi wins the world championship in a Lotus 72. Lotus win the manufacturers' championship. |
| 1978 | Mario Andretti wins the world championship with a ground-effect Lotus 79. Lotus win the manufacturers' championship. |
| 1981 | Twin-chassis Lotus 88 grand prix car is banned from Formula One racing. |

# 1960-1970 The Dutch Grand Prix

*ZANDVOORT PROGRAMME*

HOLLAND HAS PRODUCED some major figures in motor sport, among them the talented circuit designer John Hugenholtz. With various race circuits to his name, including Suzuka and Jarama, Hugenholtz created Zandvoort among the sand dunes of his country's North Sea coast. Opened in 1949 with the Formula Libre Zandvoort Grand Prix, the circuit soon established itself as a track worthy of the world's finest drivers. Sadly there were no Dutchmen among them, because the national talent was for rallying. After some spectacular accidents, Zandvoort was dropped from the Grand Prix calendar in 1985.

## ▲ ONE-TWO WINNERS

The winner of the 1968 Dutch Grand Prix was Jackie Stewart in this Matra-Ford. His team-mate, Jean-Pierre Beltoise, fought his way up from sixteenth position on the starting grid to finish second.

## ▲ FIRST-TIME WINNER

Jim Clark drove the new Lotus 49 to victory in the 1967 Dutch Grand Prix. The car was powered by the equally new Ford DFV engine, designed by Keith Duckworth. This was a famous triumph in the new car's first competitive race.

*Alan Stacey*

*Innes Ireland*

*Stirling Moss*

## ▲ STEAMED UP

Jim Clark seemed set to win the 1968 Dutch Grand Prix in this Lotus 33-Climax V8, before a leaking water pump forced him into the pits on lap 78. He eventually finished third.

## ▶ LEADER OF THE PACK

Driving a Cooper-Climax, Jack Brabham leads the pack through Hunze Rug corner soon after the start of the 1960 Dutch Grand Prix, followed by the Lotus team of Stirling Moss, Innes Ireland, and Alan Stacey, and Jo Bonnier's BRM. Brabham went on to win the race.

*Jim Clark*

*Jack Brabham*

## ▲ CHAMPION DRIVER

Graham Hill had just won his first Formula One event at the Easter 1962 Goodwood meeting when he drove this 1.5-litre V8 BRM to his first world championship victory at Zandvoort. He went on to win the German and Italian Grands Prix to take the championship title.

## ▶ BATTLE FOR THE LEAD

Fighting for the lead in the 1966 Dutch Grand Prix, Jack Brabham's Brabham-Repco V8 moves ahead of Jim Clark's Lotus-Climax 33. Brabham was the clear winner, with Clark finishing in third place.

*Jo Bonnier*

## ▼ MATRA CHAMPION

Jackie Stewart, wearing his distinctive tartan helmet, heads for victory in the 1969 Dutch Grand Prix at Zandvoort in his Matra MS80/02. This was one of six Formula One Grand Prix wins for Stewart that season, which gave him his first world championship.

### ZANDVOORT

START/FINISH

During World War II, the German army had gun emplacements in the sand dunes at Zandvoort. The service roads were used as the foundation of the postwar race circuit. Zandvoort was a demanding circuit, with varying cambers and bends, plus a couple of elevation changes.

*Jack Brabham*

# 1960-1970 The Ford Marque

"THE PUBLIC THINKS nothing of a car unless it beats other racing cars", concluded Henry Ford at the beginning of his career. He realized that racing was a way to get his cars noticed. So in 1901, as he sought backing for the foundation of his own company, Ford built a twin-cylinder racing car to demonstrate his engineering skills. Throughout its history the Ford company has continued to use motor sport as a forum for promoting its cars. In doing so the company has won every major rally, recorded four victories at Le Mans, and sponsored the most successful power unit in Grand Prix history, all the while continuing to build all-purpose cars for the general public across the world.

### ▲ INDIANAPOLIS RACER

In 1935 Ford made an assault on the Indianapolis 500 with a team of V8 racers specially built by engineer Harry Miller. Hasty preparation led to the V8s' downfall, however; their exhausts passed too near to the steering boxes, melting the lubricant and causing the steering to seize.

*Hallibrand wheels with triple-eared knock-off hub nuts*

*Fixed side windows with ventilation flaps*

### ▲ RECORD-BREAKING "999"

Henry Ford's 1902 racing car "999" had a 18.9-litre four-cylinder engine but no gearbox or rear suspension. Cycle racer Barney Oldfield, who had never driven a car before, broke several records in the "999".

### ▼ SINGLE-SEATER SUCCESS

This single-seater racing Model T was fitted with a prototype Frontenac high-compression cylinder head. L.L. Corum drove it to fifth place in the 1923 Indy 500 at an average speed of 132.8 kph (82.58 mph), nearly twice the maximum speed of a road-going Ford Model T.

### ▲ UNLUCKY RACER

Henry Ford's 1905 "666" racer was based on his six-cylinder Model K. At the car's first race meeting in Florida, USA, its crankshaft broke, and Ford cut costs by living in a tent until more cash was sent for repairs.

## ▼ FAST ON THE ICE

This super Model T "999 II" was driven at nearly 174 kph (108 mph) on the ice of Lake St. Clair, near Detroit, USA, in 1912. At the same venue in 1904 Henry Ford had set a new land speed record of 147.04 kph (91.37 mph) in the original "999".

## ▲ BOB-TAIL RACER

Champion Ford driver "Speed" Hinckley's Fronty-Ford "Bob-Tail Racer" with Rajo overhead valve conversion races at the Ascot Speedway board track in California, USA, in 1927.

## ◄ SPORTING FAMILY CAR

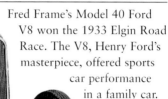

Fred Frame's Model 40 Ford V8 won the 1933 Elgin Road Race. The V8, Henry Ford's masterpiece, offered sports car performance in a family car. Its launch in 1932 led to a revival of interest in road racing.

*Door opening into roof for easier cockpit access*

*Filler cap for sill-mounted fuel cell*

B. BELL

89

### RACING HIGHLIGHTS

**1901** Henry Ford builds a 26-hp racing car and beats a 40-hp racer driven by leading manufacturer Alexander Winton.

**1904** Driving the "999", Henry Ford sets a new land speed record of 147.04 kph (91.37 mph).

**1909** A Model T wins the 6,462-km (4,016-mile) New York–Seattle race.

**1923** L.L. Corum's single-seater Ford T is fifth at the Indianapolis 500.

**1960** Jim Clark's Lotus-Ford wins a 10-lap Formula Junior race at Goodwood, the first victory for the Cosworth-modified 105E Anglia engine.

**1965** A twin-cam Lotus-Ford driven by Jim Clark wins the Indianapolis 500.

**1966** Miles and Ruby's GT40 wins the Daytona 24-hour race.

**1966** Ford sign $100,000 contract with Cosworth to develop a new Formula One engine.

**1966** Graham Hill, driving a Lola-Ford, is the first "rookie" to win the Indy 500 since 1927.

**1966** The first Le Mans victory for the Ford GT40; Mark IIs finish 1-2-3.

**1967** The Ford-Cosworth DFV Grand Prix engine wins its first race, the Dutch Grand Prix.

**1967** A Ford GT40 Mark IV driven by Gurney and Foyt wins Le Mans.

**1968** A Ford GT40 #1075 driven by Rodriguez and Bianchi wins Le Mans.

**1969** The fourth Le Mans victory for the Ford GT.

## ▲ TRIPLE VICTOR

The GT40 – just 100 cm (40 in) in height – was powered by a rear-mounted Ford V8 engine and proved to be the fastest racing coupé in the world. The car came out of Ford's Advanced Vehicles division, set up in 1963 to develop a racer capable of winning Le Mans. Ford's investment was rewarded when GT40s were placed first, second, and third in the 1966 Le Mans.

## ▲ AND AGAIN

Ford's second Le Mans victory in 1967 was achieved by the new Mk IV GT, which had a bonded aluminium honeycomb hull and 500-bhp 7-litre engine. The winning car was driven by Dan Gurney and A.J. Foyt.

# 1970-1980

# GROUND-EFFECT AND AERODYNAMICS

THE 1970s SAW much tragedy on and off the track, but they also heralded a new era in car design, with the most ingenious chassis engineers exploring every possibility in the quest for the ideal car with better handling. Once again, the impetus came from the brilliant Colin Chapman of Lotus, who had been the catalyst behind the major changes of the previous decade. With a background in aeronautical engineering, Chapman produced the first "ground-effect" racer whose design brought the body of the car closer to the track, giving huge reserves of cornering power. By the end of the decade, ground-effect cars were dominating the Formula One scene, although not all of them proved successful. Even less successful were experiments with six-wheeled racers, intended to reduce frontal area and improve cornering. The appearance of cars changed rapidly as constructors and racing authorities fought a battle of wits. Grand Prix racing was enlivened by the debut of American marques for the first time in years, and American driver Mario Andretti made a great impact on Formula One.

◄ **RACE VENUE**
Brands Hatch was a major racetrack during the 1970s. Although its tight, twisty circuit was unsuited to the Formula One cars of the late 1980s, it is still an exciting race circuit.

▼ **LOBSTER CLAW**
Ron Tauranac's split-radiator Brabham BT34 "Lobster Claw" was driven to victory in the 1971 International Trophy at Silverstone.

# 1970-1980 Racing at Brands Hatch

BRANDS HATCH PROGRAMME

THE ORIGINS OF racing at Brands Hatch in Kent go back to the 1930s, when motorcycle grass-track meetings were held on this undulating site. A hard-surfaced track was developed progressively after World War II from an original airfield perimeter track, and the circuit achieved full Grand Prix status in 1964. Brands Hatch was the venue for the British Grand Prix in alternate years from 1964 until 1987. The race was then awarded to Silverstone for an extended period because the tight and twisty Brands Hatch circuit had become unsuitable for the new generation of Formula One racing cars.

▲ ALL-NEW FERRARI

Carlos Reutemann in his Ferrari T3 leads the pack into Paddock Bend in the 1978 British Grand Prix. A completely new design for the 1978 season, the Ferrari T3 shared only its flat-12 engine and transverse gearbox with the previous T2.

▲ SUGAR POWER

Designed by Richard Divila, the sleek Copersucar FD04 was Ford DFV-powered, and had a Hewland transmission. Copersucar was the name of the Brazilian sugar marketing board which financed the car. Emerson Fittipaldi drove it to sixth place in the 1976 British Grand Prix.

## BRANDS HATCH

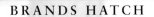

START/FINISH

Although used for motorcycle grass-track racing before World War II, Brands Hatch did not host its first car meeting until 1950. Achieving Grand Prix status in the 1960s, Brands became a major venue in the 1970s.

▲ CONTROVERSIAL WIN

Niki Lauda's Ferrari 312 T2 leads the McLaren-Ford M23 of James Hunt during the 1976 British Grand Prix. Lauda started in pole position, but Hunt took the lead on lap 45 and won the race, only to be disqualified later after an enquiry into a first-lap pile-up.

▲ FIRST-LAP DISASTER

The Ferrari 312 T2s of Niki Lauda and team-mate Clay Regazzoni went into Paddock Bend side-by-side on the first lap of the 1976 British Grand Prix, and touched. Lauda shot into the lead while Regazzoni spun out of the race.

## ▼ CHAMPION CAR

Like most successful Grand Prix cars of its day, the McLaren M23 relied on Ford power. In only its second season, 1974, the M23 took the world constructors' championship for McLaren.

*James Hunt*

## ▲ DEFLATED HOPES

Jody Scheckter's Tyrrell-Ford wins the 1974 British Grand Prix. The Ferrari 312B3 driven by Niki Lauda had been leading the race when one of the rear tyres started to deflate. Lauda was forced into the pits on the penultimate lap, allowing Scheckter through.

## ▲ TIGHT CORNER

The tight circuit at Brands Hatch was ideally suited to the all-new Ferrari T3 introduced for the 1978 season. Its chassis was designed by Mauro Forghieri to suit the new Michelin belted radial tyres. Carlos Reutemann used the car's cornering ability to win the race.

*Niki Lauda*

*Clay Regazzoni*

## ▶ WINNING DESIGN

The 1972 British Grand Prix at Brands Hatch saw one of the five Grand Prix victories of Emerson Fittipaldi in the Lotus 72 that season. The Lotus 72 was the first black and gold "John Player Special" car. It won 20 Grands Prix between 1970 and 1975.

# 1970-1980 Ferrari 312T4

THE WIDE FLAT-12 engine of the Ferrari 312 left the company at a disadvantage when it came to developing a ground-effect chassis. There was no room below the car to create the clear air passages that produced the suction that gave its V-engined rivals such remarkable traction. The 312T4 corrected many of the faults of the 312T3, which had preceded it, making use of aerodynamic bodywork and a curved nosewing to increase downforce. The car made its debut in the third race of the 1979 season, the South African Grand Prix at Kyalami. After torrential rain had delayed the start of the race, Gilles Villeneuve drove the new car to a brilliant first-time-out victory.

### ▲ DOUBLE WINNER

This Ferrari 312T4 gave Jody Scheckter the Formula One drivers' championship in 1979, with his team-mate Gilles Villeneuve finishing as runner-up. Ferrari took the constructors' championship, the Italian marque's fourth victory in five years.

### ◄ DURABLE DESIGN

The 2991cc flat-12 engine of the 312T4 was a long-lived and reliable design that had first appeared in 1969. It achieved peak power at an impressive 12,300 rpm.

### ▼ COMPROMISED AERODYNAMICS

Ferrari's flat-12 engine hampered underbody airflow. The aerodynamic bodywork and nose of the 312T4 represents the Ferrari factory's best endeavour to overcome this problem, which they sought to sidestep by relying on their customary superb car preparations alied to the powerful engine, reliable transmission and Michelin tyres.

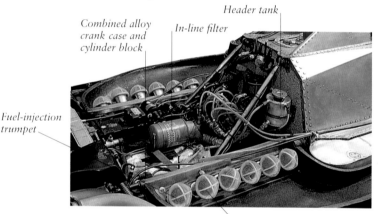

Combined alloy crank case and cylinder block

In-line filter

Header tank

Fuel-injection trumpet

Intake trumpet

Side panel to channel air over the wing

Quick-release, centre-lock wheels

Cowl conceals electrical and injection equipment

Roll bar

Light fibreglass body shell containing fuel tank

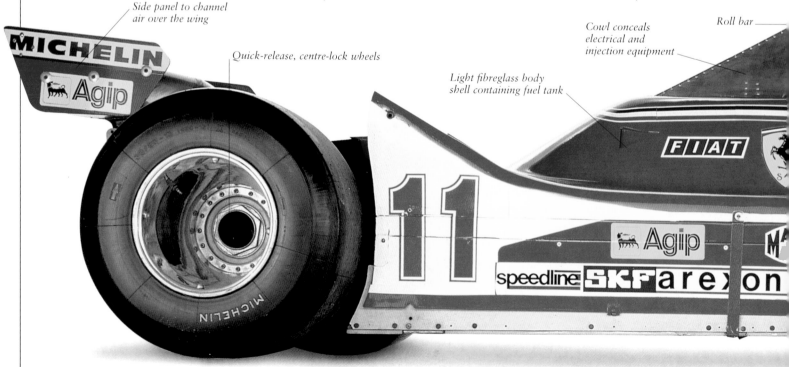

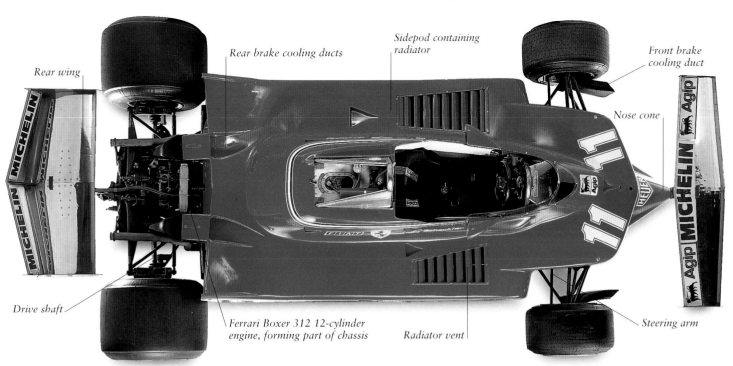

Rear wing

Rear brake cooling ducts

Sidepod containing radiator

Front brake cooling duct

Nose cone

Drive shaft

Ferrari Boxer 312 12-cylinder engine, forming part of chassis

Radiator vent

Steering arm

TOP VIEW

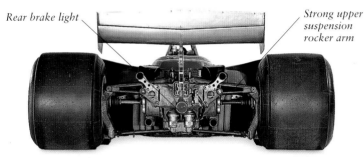

Rear brake light

Strong upper suspension rocker arm

REAR VIEW

Rear-view mirror

Roll bar

FRONT VIEW

## ▲ CONTROVERSIAL LOOKS

With its wide body and tiny tapered nose cone, the T4 has little in common with its predecessor, the T3. The front wing proved essential to the car's roadholding, while its ultra-reliable engine and transmission were a major factor in its 1979 championship win.

### SPECIFICATION

| | | | |
|---|---|---|---|
| **Chassis** | monocoque | **Weight** | 590 kg (1,300 lb) |
| **Engine** | 3.0-litre flat-12 | **Suspension** | rocker arms and coil springs (front) |
| **Valve type** | two inlet, two exhaust; twin overhead camshafts on either bank | | links and coil springs (rear) |
| **Transmission** | transverse five-speed | **Top speed** | 275 kph (170 mph) |
| **Power output** | 515 bhp | **Fuel** | petrol |

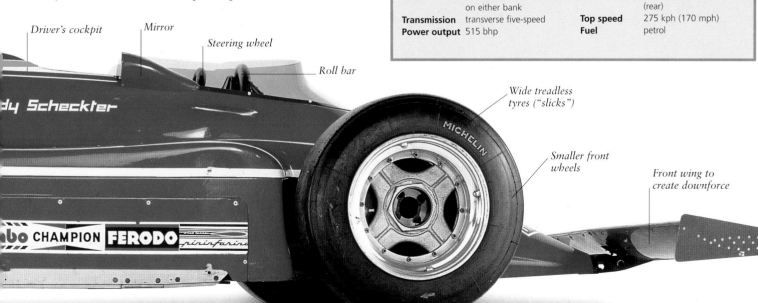

Driver's cockpit

Mirror

Steering wheel

Roll bar

Wide treadless tyres ("slicks")

Smaller front wheels

Front wing to create downforce

# 1970-1980 Racing in Belgium

*ZOLDER GRAND PRIX PROGRAMME*

ONE AMONG EUROPE'S many challenging racetracks, Belgium's Spa-Francorchamps circuit was first used in 1924 for a 24-hour race. A Grand Prix followed the next year. In the 1930s, Spa saw both triumph and tragedy for Mercedes-Benz; they won two classic Grands Prix, but they lost driver Dick Seaman in a fiery crash in 1939. The 24-hour race became a touring-car event after World War II. Difficult internal politics in 1970 caused the Belgian Grand Prix to move to Nivelles near Brussels and then to Zolder in Flemish-speaking northwest Belgium. In 1983 the Grand Prix returned to Spa.

## ▲ WINNING CAPRI

Hans Stuck Junior drove the winning 3-litre V6 Ford Capri RS with Jochen Mass in the 1972 Spa 24-hour race. It was one of the eight European and nine German wins for the successful 20-year-old Stuck, son of the famous prewar Auto Union driver.

## ▶ ANNUAL HIGHLIGHT

This is the start of the 1976 Spa 24-hour race, won by the BMW driven by Jean-Marie Detrin and Nico Denuth. Deemed "the best event of the year" by enthusiasts, the race was revived in 1964 after an 11-year interval.

## ▲ REACHING A PEAK

Frenchman Didier Pironi revived the flagging fortunes of the Ligier team in 1980 by driving this Ligier-Ford to victory at Zolder. But it was only a temporary reprieve; faced by strong opposition from Williams and Ferrari, the team pulled out of Grand Prix racing at the end of the season and did not return until 1983.

## ▲ LOTUS-FORD REVOLUTIONARY

The 1977 Belgian Grand Prix was won by the Swedish driver Gunnar Nilsson in this revolutionary ground-effect Lotus-Ford 78. He finished 14 seconds ahead of Niki Lauda's Ferrari. This was to be the highlight of Nilsson's tragically brief career which was cut short by cancer in 1978.

## ▲ HARVEY POSTLETHWAITE DESIGN

This Harvey Postlethwaite-designed 308C was driven at Zolder in 1976 by Harold Ertl as part of the Hesketh team. The car had to retire due to engine failure. Ertl had replaced James Hunt who secured Hesketh's only victory in the 1975 Dutch Grand Prix.

## ▲ ULTIMATE ACHIEVEMENT

Lights ablaze, a BMW touring car hurtles into the dusk during the 1976 Spa 24-hour race, an event described as having a greater, more exciting atmosphere than Le Mans. To win at Spa in such a car is judged the ultimate achievement in that branch of motor sport.

## ▲ BAVARIAN BOMBSHELL

This is the winning BMW in the 1976 24-hour race at Spa. In the 1970s, the Spa 24-hour race was dominated by BMW and Ford. The Bavarian marque won the race six times in that decade and their rivals from Cologne – Ford – took the chequered flag in the remaining years.

## ▲ SPEEDY SUCCESS

Prepared in a Cologne competition workshop, the Weslake-Ford V6-engined Capri 3-litre, which won the 1972 24-hour race at Spa, averaged 205 kph (130 mph).

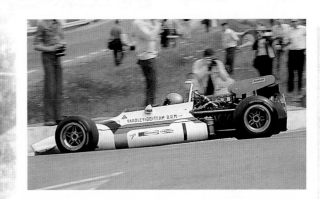

## ▲ LONG-AWAITED VICTORY

Pedro Rodriguez gave the BRM team a valuable boost by winning the 1970 Spa Grand Prix with this Tony Southgate-designed V12-engined P160. This was BRM's first Grand Prix victory since Stewart won at Monaco in 1966.

## ▲ AMERICAN CHALLENGE

Geoff Ferris was responsible for designing this Penske-Ford PC4, driven with some success by John Watson in 1976. Although Watson won in Austria, he came only seventh at Zolder.

### SPA

Originally mapped out on country roads in the Ardennes forest, the Spa circuit was rebuilt in the 1970s after being declared too dangerous. But the replacement circuit retained many of the features – such as the Eau Rouge corner – that had made the old track so appealing to racers.

START/FINISH

# 1970-1980 The Porsche Marque

PROFESSOR FERDINAND PORSCHE was an old man before the marque bearing his name came into existence in 1948. He had already had a long career as a designer and engineer. His many achievements ranged from the creation of the supercharged Mercedes sports cars of the 1920s and the Auto Union Grand Prix cars, to the Volkswagen "People's Car" of the 1930s. Ironically, the humble Volkswagen was the basis for the first Porsche sports car. Later, more sophisticated designs from the Porsche dynasty became legendary in such demanding events as Le Mans and the Targa Florio.

### ▲ TARGA WINNER

Edgar Barth and Umberto Maglioli drove this 904/8 Coupé to victory in the prototype class of the 1964 Targa Florio in Sicily. A break with Porsche tradition, the 904 had a box-frame chassis beneath a fibreglass body.

### ◄ VOLKSWAGEN AT HEART

Ferdinand Porsche's last major design was the 356 sports car. Using the basic mechanical layout of an earlier Volkswagen design, Porsche created an aerodynamic rear-engined 1100cc racer with a very low centre of gravity and pin-sharp handling.

*Air-cooling scoops*

*Dual headlamps for night section of 24-hour race*

*Air intake ducts for ventilated disc brakes*

*Central NACA duct for transmission cooling*

*Duct for cockpit-cooling air*

*Quad headlamp*

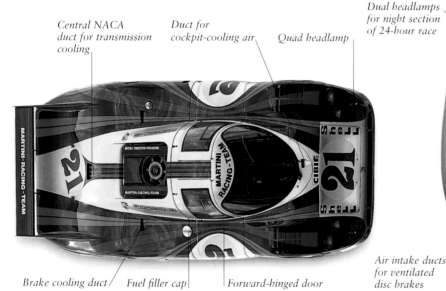

*Brake cooling duct*  *Fuel filler cap*  *Forward-hinged door*

### ▲ AERODYNAMIC AIDS

The "Langheck" version of the Porsche 917, unveiled in 1970, had a lengthened tail to improve aerodynamics and reduce fuel consumption. This 917, powered by a 4.9-litre flat-12 engine, was raced at Le Mans in 1972 by Vic Elford and Gerard Larrousse.

### ◄ GULLWING COUPÉ

The Type 906 Carrera 6 was launched in 1966 and had a similar fibreglass body to the 904, with gullwing doors. The cars had either a 210-bhp six or a 260-bhp flat-eight 2.2-litre engine. In the 1966 Le Mans, 906s finished fourth, fifth, sixth, and seventh.

### ▶ SON OF MICKEY MOUSE

Developed from a lowered version of the RS known as the "Mickey Mouse", the 1.5-litre flat-four Type 718 RSK was first seen in sports car events in 1957. It was then developed in this dual-purpose Formula Two/sports-racing guise for the 1958 season. Jean Behra won the Reims Formula Two race in 1958 in a centre-seat RSK.

### ▲ PACESETTER

The well-proven "Kurz" version of the Porsche 917 dominated the 1970 Le Mans race, with this JWA team car, driven by Jo Siffert. It set the pace in the early stages of the race. Up to 1998, Porsche had won 16 times at Le Mans.

*Single pantograph windscreen wiper arm*

*Fuel filler*

### ▲ BIRTHDAY PRESENT

Seen here in its 1997 form, the 3.2-litre GT1 was developed in response to the challenge from the far costlier McLaren Formula One. The car gave the Porsche marque its 16th victory at Le Mans in 1998. Porsche thus had good reason to celebrate on their 50th anniversary.

### RACING HIGHLIGHTS

**1948** Porsche's first racing victory, a class win in the Innsbruck City Race for the 356 driven by Porsche's nephew Herbert Kaes.

**1970** Attwood and Herrmann in a 917K gain the first Le Mans win for Porsche.

**1971** Porsche's second Le Mans win, by the 4.9-litre 917K of Helmut Marko and Gijs van Lennep, is an all-time record of 396 laps, 5,335 km (3,315 miles), 222.33 kph (138.133 mph).

**1976** Le Mans victory for the Porsche 936.

**1981** Porsche take the first of a record seven consecutive Le Mans victories.

**1984** Niki Lauda wins the Formula One drivers' championship in a McLaren-Porsche-TAG.

**1985** Alain Prost wins the Formula One drivers' championship in a McLaren-Porsche-TAG.

**1986** Alain Prost wins the Formula One drivers' championship in a McLaren-Porsche-TAG.

**1996** A TWR-Porsche WSC95 wins Le Mans.

**1997** A TWR-Porsche WSC95 wins Le Mans.

**1998** A Porsche 3.2-litre GT1 wins Le Mans.

### ▲ REDUCED FRONTAL AREA

Developed from the 910, the Type 907 was first seen at Le Mans in 1967. The car had a reduced frontal area and right-hand drive so that drivers were able to place the car with more accuracy on a normal right-hand-direction racing circuit.

### ▶ FIRST RACER

The first Porsche developed specifically for racing was the Type 550 which appeared in spyder form in 1953. It won at the Nürburgring in May 1953. Its alloy Kommenda body was mounted on a ladder-type frame with independent torsion-bar trailing-arm front suspension and swing axles at the rear.

# 1970-1980 US Endurance Racing

DAYTONA'S LEADER BOARD

ENDURANCE RACING began in the United States. The first 24-hour contest was held in 1905, and since 1966 the home of American round-the-clock racing has been the "Trioval" Daytona International Speedway. The circuit was built in the 1950s by Bill France, a veteran of the long-established stock-car races on the Daytona Beach-Road Course, as an East Coast rival for Indianapolis. Daytona hosts one of NASCAR's greatest events, the Daytona 500, which in the 1970s saw machines such as the winged Plymouth SuperBird, Dodge Charger Daytona, Chevrolet Laguna, and Ford Thunderbird vying for supremacy.

### ▸ POWER CURVE

Les Kelly's Chevrolet Camaro powers its way through an infield turn to keep Vince Muzzin's heavily-modified Chevrolet Corvette at bay during the 1975 Camel GT race at Daytona.

Preston Henn,
Ferrari Daytona

Hoyt Overbaugh,
Chevy Monza

### ▲ STOCK JOBBERS

Driving a Chevy Monza 2+2 Coupé, Hoyt Overbaugh heads a group of sports coupés into an infield turn in the 1977 Camel GT race at Daytona. By this date, the "stock" cars competing at Daytona were specially built, using "bodies-in-white" supplied by the automakers solely for the purpose of racing.

### ▸ PONY CAR TAKES THE LEAD

Heavily modified for racing, Charlie Kemp's Ford Mustang II is first into the infield bend during the 1978 Camel GT race at Daytona. Following close behind the Mustang are a Jaguar XJ-S and two Porsche 911s.

## ▼ SPIRITED RACER

This Chevrolet Corvette Coupé "Spirit of Sebring" of Benrus Team Corvette, driven by John Greenwood and Mike Brockman, was a colourful contender in the 1976 24-Hour race at Daytona.

*Eye-catching livery*

*Spoiler*

## ▲ CHEVY CHASERS

The Chevrolet Camaro Sport Coupé of Herb Jones and Steve Faul, followed by a Corvette and a Porsche 911, leads the pack around one of the high-banked turns in the 1976 24-hour race at Daytona.

## ▲ RACING BUICK

Gene Felton drives his Buick Skylark sedan in the 1977 Camel GT race. Usually regarded as typical family transportation, the Buick marque is, in fact, one of the oldest names in American stock-car racing.

## ▶ PIT STOP

This is the Chevy Corvette driven in the 1977 Camel GT at Daytona by Phil Currin. The Chevrolet company takes its name from Swiss-born Louis Chevrolet one of the great pioneer American racing drivers.

## ▼ WINGS AND WHEELS

Glenn Bunch drove this Dodge Challenger, powered by a muscular 426 cu in hemi-head V8 engine and fitted with a prominent rear wing spoiler, in the 1978 Camel GT race at Daytona.

*Power bulge*

## DAYTONA

START/FINISH

The pride of the Daytona Beach area, the 4-km (2.5-mile) Trioval speedway curls around a lake on 1.53 hectares (377 acres) of former swampland. The infield loop and the optional chicane supplement the high-speed banked oval for sports-car racing.

THE 69th • MAY 26, 1985

INDIANAPOLIS
500

"An Image of Victory"

# 1980 · 1990

# THE REIGN OF THE TURBOCHARGERS

Performance reached an all-time high in the mid-1980s. Power outputs rose to unprecedented levels as engine designers learned to control the awesome forces unleashed by turbocharging. The advent of sophisticated electronic controls manipulating fuel injection and ignition through on-board computers made it all possible, keeping the tiny 1.5-litre turbocharged engines balanced on the critical knife-edge between maximum boost and total destruction. Again, it was a battle between the technicians and the regulators. Limits on tyre sizes and the amount of ground force that could be developed meant that engine outputs which regularly exceeded 1000 bhp, and could even go beyond 1250 bhp, tested the roadholding abilities of the car chassis to the utmost. This situation could not be allowed to continue, particularly when top speeds of over 320 kph (200 mph) were being attained, coupled with awesome acceleration. New rules dramatically reduced turbo boost, and after four dramatic seasons, the thunderous reign of the Grand Prix turbos was brought to an end.

◀ **AMERICAN CLASSIC**

The programme for the 1985 Indianapolis 500 evokes the ghosts of races past. The classic American race was first run in 1911.

▼ **FORZA FERRARI**

Ferrari's 1985 156/85 was the first turbocharged racer to reach the 1000 bhp barrier, although a more realistic 880 bhp was achieved during racing.

# 1980-1990 The French Grand Prix

PAUL RICARD
FINISHING LINE

A NEW GENERATION of Grand Prix circuits had been built during the 1960s, and by the late 1980s the finest circuit was the Paul Ricard facility in Provence. The French Grand Prix was given to this new track in preference to its rival at Dijon-Prenois. This fine French track had a driver to match in Alain Prost, who drove his McLaren to the championship in 1985, 1986, and 1989. However, the 1990s saw the Paul Ricard circuit unseated by a new track at Magny-Cours, which was upgraded to Grand Prix standard with the support of the then French President François Mitterand.

*Push-pull rod suspension*

*Slotted rear wing*

### ▲ LIMITED BUDGET

Without a major sponsor, Tyrrell faced 1982 on a limited budget. However, the basic design of their Ford-powered 011 was extensively revised, with updated aerodynamics and push-pull rod suspension. Michele Alboreto finished sixth at the Ricard circuit, but ended the season with victory in Las Vegas, USA, Tyrrell's first win since 1978.

### ▲ THWARTED CHALLENGE

Thierry Boutsen in the Benetton-Ford B187 posed a strong challenge to Ayrton Senna's Lotus-Honda in the early stages of the 1987 French Grand Prix at Paul Ricard. However, Boutsen's car was withdrawn on lap 31 with a failed distributor drive.

*Alain Prost, Renault-Elf RE30B*

*Fuel tank cowl and engine cover*

*Sliding skirt*

### ▲ PROBLEM AERODYNAMICS

Gilles Villeneuve drives the turbocharged V6-engined Ferrari 126CK during the French Grand Prix at Paul Ricard in 1981. Troublesome sliding-skirt aerodynamics had given Villeneuve problems, and he crashed during practice for the race.

### ▲ SUCCESSFUL UPDATE

Alain Prost drives the Renault-Elf RE30B to second place in the 1982 French Grand Prix at Paul Ricard. The car was an updated version of the 1981 design with a stiffer, lighter monocoque and revised suspension. Its twin-turbocharged V6 engine was uprated to 550 bhp.

## ▼ TURBOCHARGED WINNER

Alain Prost drove this McLaren-Honda MP4/4 in the 1988 French Grand Prix. The MP4/4 had a 1.5-litre V6 engine and was the last of the turbocharged McLaren-Hondas. Although Prost's team-mate Ayrton Senna was the favourite to win the race, he was held back by gearbox problems, and Prost beat him into second place.

## ▲ WINNING ON HOME GROUND

Local knowledge paid off in the 1983 French Grand Prix at Paul Ricard, because the eventual winner, Alain Prost in a Renault EF1, had trained at the Paul Ricard racing school in the early 1970s, and thus knew every nuance of the tricky circuit.

## ▲ UNHAPPY BIRTHDAY

Riccardo Patrese started from second position on the grid in this turbocharged Brabham-BMW in the 1983 French Grand Prix. It was his 29th birthday, so the omens looked good. But he retired on the 19th lap with an overheating engine after losing all the coolant from the radiator.

*Niki Lauda,*
*McLaren-Ford MP4B*

## ▼ EARLY EXIT

Andrea de Cesaris drove this Alfa Romeo Tipo 182 in the 1982 French Grand Prix, but crashed on the 27th lap. The Tipo – a Ducourage design produced by the Autodelta factory – had a carbon-fibre honeycomb chassis and was powered by Alfa's ageing V12 power unit.

*New bodywork for 1982*

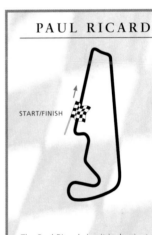

## PAUL RICARD

START/FINISH

The Paul Ricard circuit is dominated by the mile-long Mistral straight, which feeds into the flat-out Signes curve. The straight was shortened in the late 1980s after Elio de Angelis was killed in a crash during practice.

## ▲ OFF TO A BAD START

The 1987 French Grand Prix at Paul Ricard began in confusion after Andrea de Cesaris in his Brabham collided with a McLaren. The race was eventually won by Nigel Mansell's Williams-Honda FW11B.

# 1980-1990 Jaguar XJR-9LM

THE DEVELOPMENT of the successful Jaguar XJR-9LM began in 1985 when Jaguar approved the building of a new car to contest Le Mans. Team leader Tom Walkinshaw had already begun building the new XJR-6 racer designed by Tony Southgate. This new Jaguar was truly state-of-the-art, with a chassis composed entirely of Kevlar and carbon fibre materials, while its ingeniously shaped bulkhead permitted the long V12 engine to be mounted as far forward as possible in the interests of weight distribution. The 1985 and 1986 seasons proved the potential of the new endurance Jaguar, and in 1987 an improved XJR-8 made an unsuccessful attempt on Le Mans. In 1988 the aerodynamically superior XJR-9LM scored a victory in the classic 24-hour race.

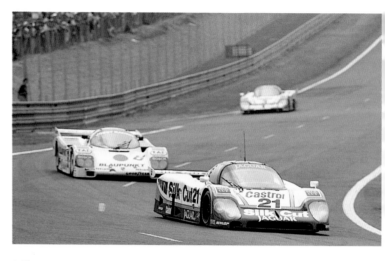

### ▲ CHAMPIONSHIP YEAR

In 1988 the XJR-9LM, seen here in the lead, achieved Jaguar's sixth win at Le Mans, and also won the world sports car championship. It had taken only two seasons for Jaguar to undermine Porsche's supremacy in sports-prototype racing.

*7-litre V12 engine*

*Inboard suspension dampers*

### ◀ POWERFUL ALTERNATIVE

Jaguar used this 7-litre version of their proven V12 engine for Le Mans, but in the United States, where Jaguar's Group 44 racing team raced the American-developed Jaguar XJR-5 and XJR-7, a smaller 620-bhp 6-litre power unit was used.

*Rear wing*

*Telemetry and communications antennae*

*Moulded windscreen*

### ▼ IMPROVING THE AIRFLOW

By using smaller wheel rims at the back, designer Tony Southgate lowered the rear bodywork of the XJR-9 compared with the XJR-8, improving airflow over the rear wing.

*Detachable nose section*

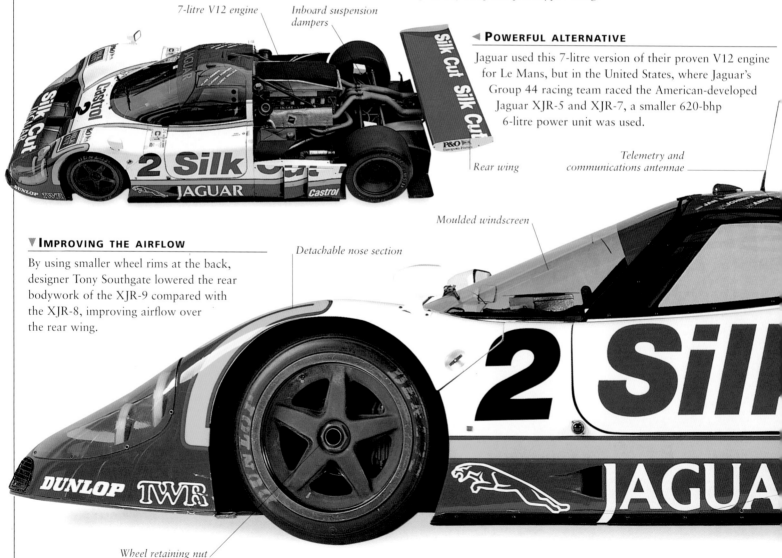

*Wheel retaining nut*

*Headlights for night racing* · *Aerodynamic tail* · *17-in (43-cm) wheel* · *Under-car venturi passage* · *Transmission*

FRONT VIEW        SIDE VIEW        REAR VIEW

## ◢ DOWNFORCE

The bodywork of the racing Jaguars was designed to achieve a high level of downforce. The V12 engine configuration enabled the incorporation of underbody airflow passages, giving the cars a considerable advantage over their opponents.

*Air scoop*

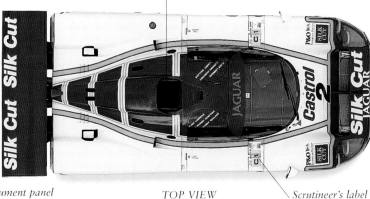

TOP VIEW

*Instrument panel*

*Ergonomic driving seat*

*Scrutineer's label*

## ◢ DESIGNED FOR ENDURANCE

Driver comfort is paramount at Le Mans, the most demanding race of its kind. The cockpit of an endurance racer such as the XJR-9LM is comprehensively instrumented to alert the driver to the car's condition.

### SPECIFICATION

| | |
|---|---|
| **Chassis** | carbon fibre/Kevlar tub |
| **Engine** | 7.0 litres V12 |
| **Valve type** | one inlet, one exhaust; one camshaft per bank |
| **Transmission** | TWR/March five-speed gearbox transaxle final drive |
| **Power output** | 720 bhp |
| **Weight** | 850 kg (1,874 lb) |
| **Suspension** | push-rod and inboard coil spring/damper (front) coil and wishbone (rear) |
| **Top speed** | 220 mph (350 kph ) |
| **Fuel** | petrol |

## ▼ FIT TO RACE

The scrutineer's label attached to the car confirms that it has been inspected and passed as being fit to race. The racing category is indicated by the code on the label made up of a letter and a number.

*Filler for 100-litre (22-gallon) fuel tank*

*Endplate allows adjustments of wing*

*Rear wing*

*Enclosed rear wheel to maximize venturi effect beneath car*

*Air intake*    *NACA duct*

# 1980-1990 The McLaren Marque

THE TEAM FOUNDED by racing driver Bruce McLaren entered Formula One racing in 1966 with the M2B. This car, designed by Robin Herd, had a novel stressed-skin hull formed by a sandwich of balsa wood between aluminium. Despite the death of Bruce McLaren in 1970, the marque has continued to produce cars of exceptional technical interest. McLaren have used Ford, TAG-Porsche, Honda, and Peugeot power, but in 1995 the company entered a long-term partnership with Mercedes-Benz for the supply of engines. The marque dominated the 1980s and has won the Formula One Constructors' Championship eight times. McLaren also gained a well-deserved victory at Le Mans with their Formula One supercar.

▲ **McLaren's champion**

Three-times world champion Niki Lauda sits in the centre of the pack in his McLaren-TAG MP4/2B during the 1985 Australian Grand Prix. The car was an updated version of the one in which Lauda had won the 1984 world championship. Lauda withdrew after his car spun off the track, and the race marked his retirement.

▲ **Winner first time**

McLaren switched to the new Ford DFV engine as soon as it became generally available in 1968. The engine was fitted in this McLaren M7A, which won its first event, the non-championship Race of Champions.

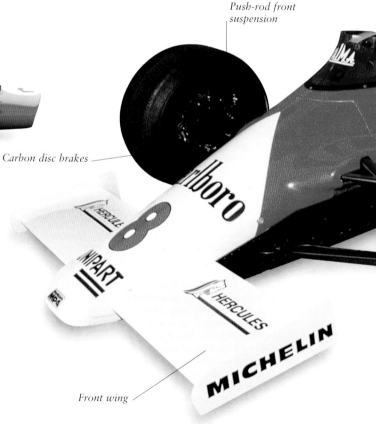

*Push-rod front suspension*

*Carbon disc brakes*

*Front wing*

▲ **Computer trouble**

Ayrton Senna drives the new McLaren MP4/4, powered by the Honda RA168-E engine, in the 1988 Spanish Grand Prix. Misled by a faulty computerized fuel gauge, Senna lost time and only finished fourth while team-mate Alain Prost cruised home to victory.

▲ **Last of the line**

The 1984 MP4/1C marked the end of McLaren's long association with the Ford DFV engine, which had given the McLaren International team a memorable maiden victory in the 1981 British Grand Prix. The Ford engine was succeeded by the new Porsche turbo-charged TAG engine.

## ▲ AERODYNAMIC EXCELLENCE

Designed to meet demanding new regulations introduced for 1998 to reduce the potential performance of Formula One racers, the McLaren-Mercedes MP4/13 makes full use of aerodynamic solutions.

*Extended headrest*

*Integral front wing*

*Engine air intake*

*Wide body*

## ▲ HONEYCOMB CHASSIS

This honeycomb-chassis McLaren-Ford M26, which succeeded the M23 during 1977, was driven by James Hunt, seen here at the British Grand Prix. Hunt only managed fifth place in the world championship despite his victory the previous year with the four-year-old M23.

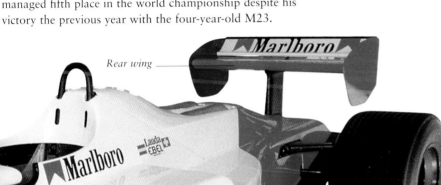

*Rear wing*

*Carbon-fibre bodywork*

*Magnesium wheels*

## ▲ SWELLING FLANKS

With its flat-topped nose and "Coke-bottle" contours, the Ford-powered McLaren M19 featured an innovative "rising-rate" suspension system. It took Denny Hulme to third place in the world championship in 1972.

## ▼ LE MANS WINNER

The Formula One GTR was a racing version of McLaren's 370-kph (230-mph) M1 road car. Powered by a 630-bhp 6.1-litre BMW V12 engine, it won its first Le Mans in 1995.

## ◄ WOODEN WONDER

With its hull of Malite aluminium sandwiching a balsa-wood core, the Serenissima V8-powered 1966 M2B reflected contemporary aircraft design. Driven here in the British Grand Prix by Bruce McLaren, it finished sixth.

### RACING HIGHLIGHTS

| | |
|---|---|
| 1966 | Formula One debut for McLaren at the Monaco Grand Prix. |
| 1974 | McLaren's first drivers' and constructors' championships are won by Emerson Fittipaldi in the Ford-powered M23. |
| 1976 | James Hunt wins the drivers' championship in his Marlboro McLaren-Ford M23. |
| 1984 | The new Marlboro McLaren-TAG Turbo MP4/2 wins 12 out of 18 races and both drivers' and constructors' championships. |
| 1985 | The drivers' and constructors' championships are won by Alain Prost's MP4/2B. |
| 1986 | Prost wins a drivers' championship in his Marlboro McLaren-TAG Turbo MP4/2C. |
| 1988 | Now with Porsche power, McLaren win a record 15 out of 16 races. |
| 1990 | The drivers' and constructors' championships are won by Ayrton Senna's McLaren-Honda. |
| 1991 | The drivers' and constructors' championships are again won by Ayrton Senna's McLaren-Honda. |
| 1993 | McLaren becomes Formula One's most successful marque, beating Ferrari's record. |
| 1995 | The McLaren Formula One car wins the Le Mans 24-hour race at the first attempt. |
| 1998 | The drivers' and constructors' championships are won by Mika Hakkinen's McLaren Mercedes (MP4/13). |

# 1980-1990 Lola Chevy

THE INDIANAPOLIS 500 of 1990 saw the fastest qualifying speed exceed 360 kph (225 mph) for the first time. Not surprisingly, the winning Chevy-Indy-powered Lola driven by Arie Luyendyk finished at an all-time record average of 299.25 kph (186 mph), taking just 2 hours, 41 minutes, and 18.4 seconds to cover 500 miles. Although the engine bore the Chevrolet "bow-tie" emblem, it was really a second-generation Cosworth designed by two former Cosworth employees, Mario Ilien and Paul Morgan, backed by money from Chevrolet and Penske. The Lola chassis, like that of every other car on the grid, was built in England at a cost of around £143,000 ($250,000).

**DIGITAL DASHBOARD DISPLAY**

### ▲ SMART TACTICS

Arie Luyendyk speeds towards victory in his Lola Chevy at the 1990 Indianapolis 500. Luyendyk made a pitstop while the other racers were slowing for a yellow flag, indicating a hazard. This meant that he lost very little ground to other competitors, which contributed to his win.

### ▼ SHAPED IN THE WIND TUNNEL

The Lola Chevy features ground-effect underwings which create a turbulent wake behind the car, foiling the drivers of following cars who would otherwise benefit from an aerodynamic "tow" in the car's slipstream.

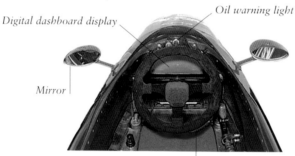

Digital dashboard display

Oil warning light

Mirror

Detachable steering wheel with "push-to-talk" radio control button

### ◄ DIGITAL DISPLAY

Luyendyk's Lola Chevy features a digital dashboard display, controlled from an onboard "black box" that displays such vital information as turboboost, fuel flow, and engine revolutions. The big red light warns of oil-pressure loss.

Rear wing

Aerodynamic shaping to divert airflow on to rear wing

Intake trumpet

Chevy Indy V8 engine

Endplate allows adjustment of wing

Wheel retaining nut

Push rod

Fuel overflow
hose connection

Suspension
arm

Fuel hose
connection

Pylon-mounted
rear wing

**TOP VIEW**

## SPECIFICATION

| | |
|---|---|
| Chassis | Kevlar/carbonfibre/ aluminium honeycomb composite |
| Engine | 2.65-litre V8 |
| Valve type | two inlet, two exhaust; two camshafts per block |
| Transmission | two speed |
| Power output | 750 bhp |
| Weight | 725 kg (1,600 lb) |
| Suspension | double wishbone (front) double wishbone (rear) |
| Top speed | 370 kph (230 mph) |
| Fuel | methanol |

◀ **TAILOR-MADE WINNER**

Though two-thirds of the entrants in the 1990 Indianapolis 500 were Lolas, every one differed in detail, because each team modified their cars to suit their own individual preferences regarding wings, spring settings, air ducts, and engine details.

Nose cone

Fuel inlet

**SIDE VIEW**

Streamlined
control arm for
optimum airflow

Rollcage

Radio aerial

Transaxle

Ground-effect
expansion cone

**FRONT VIEW**

**REAR VIEW**

Carbon fibre
composite body

Air intake for underwings

Goodyear Eagle race tyres
(four sets needed per race)

Front wing
end tab

# 1980-1990 The Spanish Grand Prix

*AYRTON SENNA WINS, 1986*

FORMULA ONE REACHED an all-time high in the 1980s with the advent of sophisticated electronic controls to regulate turbocharged engines. The Spanish Grand Prix, however, did not enjoy such a renaissance. The race moved to Jarama in the early 1980s when the rival Montjuich circuit was abandoned for safety reasons. Jarama was not much more successful; it held its last Grand Prix in 1981 and Formula One seemed lost to Spain. Even the 1986 Jerez circuit, which boasts splendid facilities, has failed to draw large crowds due to its isolated location. The few races that Spain saw in the 1980s were dominated, as elsewhere, by Williams and Ferrari.

### ▲ EASILY A WINNER

In 1980, Jarama was the arena for a struggle between motor sport's controlling body FISA and FOCA, the Formula One Constructors' Association. FISA declared the Spanish Grand Prix illegal and Renault, Alfa, and Ferrari abstained, leaving Ford-Cosworth-powered racers to contest a race easily won by Alan Jones's Saudia-Leyland Williams.

*Larger front wing endplate for improved aerodynamics*

*Slimmed-down upper body to improve airflow over rear wing*

### ▲ SPANISH FOURTH

Nelson Piquet finished first in the 1987 championship. He only came fourth, however, in the 1987 Spanish Grand Prix at Jerez in this 950 hp turbocharged Williams-Honda FW11B.

*Radiators in sidepods*

*One-piece Kevlar bodywork*

*Gilles Villeneuve*

### ▲ NEW IMPROVED LOTUS-RENAULT

This Lotus-Renault 98T with which Ayrton Senna won at Jerez in 1986 is an updated version of the turbocharged 1985–1986 97T with improved aerodynamics and hydraulic ride-height adjusters which automatically compensate for fuel-load lightening.

### ▲ WINNING BY A WHISKER

Driving the new turbocharged Ferrari 1.5-litre V6 126C, Gilles Villeneuve makes a brilliant start in the 1981 Spanish Grand Prix at Jarama. He cut through the pack from seventh place on the grid to win by 0.22 seconds.

## ▲ PHOTO FINISH

Ayrton Senna's Lotus-Renault leads the Marlboro McLaren of Alain Prost into one of the many tight bends at Jerez during the 1986 Spanish Grand Prix. Senna eventually won the race by 0.014 seconds from Nigel Mansell's Williams-Honda.

## ▼ OWN-MAKE ENGINE

Martin Brundle drove this Zakspeed 871 to 11th place in the 1987 Spanish Grand Prix, but the German company have had more success racing Ford saloons in Formula One. From 1985 to 1989 they used their own turbocharged 1.5-litre four-cylinder and carbon-fibre Kevlar monocoque cars.

## ▲ LIGIER-FORD VICTORY

The Ligier-Ford JS11, designed by Gerard Ducarouge, easily won the 1979 Spanish Grand Prix – cruising home 20 seconds clear of Carlos Reutemann's Lotus.

*John Watson*

*Carlos Reutemann*

## JARAMA

START/FINISH

Designed by Dutchman John Hugenholtz, the Jarama circuit near Madrid had to compromise to fit into too small an area of the leisure facility owned by the Royal Automobile Club of Spain. Its compromised layout meant that its Grand Prix days were always going to be numbered from the start.

## ▲ COMPUTER VICTORY

Nigel Mansell wins the 1987 Spanish Grand Prix at Jerez in his Williams-Honda – the eighth out of nine Grand Prix victories for Williams that season. Patrick Head developed a computer-controlled variable ride-height system for Williams' use in the final European Grands Prix that year.

# 1990-2000

# AN AGE OF ELECTRONIC WIZARDRY

WITH THE emphasis once again on naturally aspirated engines, the constructors and regulators engaged in a battle of wits. Rules were drawn up to exclude electronic aids such as traction control and active suspension systems that gave greater cornering power. Tyre regulations were redrawn, too, in an effort to limit racing speeds. Drivers were still allowed to talk to their pit crews via two-way radio links, and they could even download electronic data from the battery of computers that have now become an essential part of pit equipment. However, a ban was put on engineers being able to modify the behaviour of the car during the race via electronic signals from the pits. Now that Grand Prix cars have so much in common with fighter aircraft, it is inevitable that such adjuncts as on-board "black box" accident recorders and energy-absorbing impact structures have become compulsory in the continuous search for maximum driver safety.

◀ **WORLD CLASS SPORT**

At the end of the 20th century, Formula One has blossomed into one of the world's most popular sports.

▼ **LEAN PICKINGS**

Apart from a second place in Hungary in 1997, world champion Damon Hill enjoyed little success with his Yamaha-engined Arrows.

## 1990-2000 Indianapolis

IN THE LATE 1990s Indianapolis has become the focus of the new Indy Racing League (IRL) series. These races were instigated by the owner of the Indianapolis Motor Speedway, Tony Hulman George, to enable competitors with more modest budgets to remain in contention. IRL is based on a 4-litre naturally aspirated stock-block formula, and cars are limited to a cost of $385,000 (£220,000). The chassis are from Dallara and G-Force, and most of the competing cars are powered by the Olds Aurora quad-cam V8 engine. But of course the name of Indianapolis is still synonymous with the Indy 500, which attracts up to half-a-million spectators each Memorial Day holiday.

*Secret-construction radial tyre*

### ▲ THE CHIPS ARE DOWN

Eddie Cheever competed in the 1998 Indy 500 in his V8 Aurora-powered Dallara. He had started in 33 Formula One contests without winning a single one, and only found a sponsor – Rachel's Potato Chips – a week before the race. But he won after leading for 76 laps.

### ◀ KEEPING IT IN THE FAMILY

Al Unser Senior, pictured here in 1972 with his Parnelli-Offy, designed by Maurice Phillipe, is one of only two drivers to have won the Indianapolis 500 four times. His son, Al Unser Jr, won in 1994 driving a Penske-Mercedes, and three other members of the Unser family have also won the race.

### ▶ READY FOR A FLYING START

In front of a capacity crowd, Billy Boat lines up his Conseco/A.J. Foyt for the start of the 1998 Indy 500. Greg Ray's Thomas Knapp Motorsports entry is to his right and Kenny Brack's Dallara-Aurora is on the outside.

*Kenny Brack, Dallara Aurora*

*Greg Ray, Thomas Knapp Motorsprots*

## ▼ OUT OF CONTENTION

Billy Boat started in pole position in the Conseco/A. J. Foyt in the 1998 Indy 500 and led for the first dozen laps, but he dropped out of contention when his car's transmission jammed.

*Adjustable wing for downforce*

*Streamlined upper and lower control arms*

## ▲ LOLA FOUND WANTING

These three Lola T93/00 cars were strong contenders in the 1993 Indy 500. Mario Andretti, in the centre, led for 72 laps out of 200, but another Indy veteran, Emerson Fittipaldi, won in a Penske-Chevrolet, with Andretti fifth.

*Air intake*  *Knock-off hubcap*

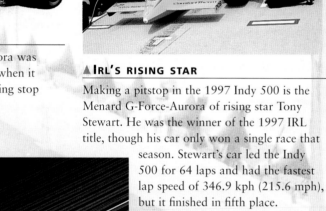

## ▲ THIRST COSTS FIRST

Swedish driver Kenny Brack's V8 Dallara-Aurora was leading on the 87th lap of the 1998 Indy 500 when it began to run low on fuel. The resulting refuelling stop dropped Brack down to sixth position.

## ▲ IRL'S RISING STAR

Making a pitstop in the 1997 Indy 500 is the Menard G-Force-Aurora of rising star Tony Stewart. He was the winner of the 1997 IRL title, though his car only won a single race that season. Stewart's car led the Indy 500 for 64 laps and had the fastest lap speed of 346.9 kph (215.6 mph), but it finished in fifth place.

*Billy Boat, co/A. J. Foyt*

## ▲ DEEP PURPLE

Jimmy Kite drove the exotically named Royal Purple Synthetic/Synertec for Team Scandia in the 1998 Indy 500. From 26th place on the grid, Kite worked his way through the field to finish 11th.

## INDIANAPOLIS

START/FINISH

The layout of the Indianapolis Motor Speedway is the same as it was in 1911, though the track has been upgraded to cope with speeds of up to 390 kph (240 mph) and only a token strip of bricks remains to recall the old "Brickyard". It is planned to develop a Grand Prix circuit there.

# 1990-2000 The Japanese Grand Prix

*SUZUKA PROGRAMME*

ALTHOUGH THE SUZUKA circuit opened for international racing as long ago as 1962, the first Japanese Grands Prix were held at Fuji in 1976 and 1977. The race was not run again for a decade, and when it was revived in 1987, Suzuka was chosen as the venue. The circuit is owned by the Honda company, and was originally a test track. Suzuka was the scene of two famous clashes between arch-rivals Alain Prost and Ayrton Senna. In 1989, their McLaren-Hondas collided when Prost refused to allow Senna to pass. The following year, already leading the championship, Senna rammed Prost's Ferrari off the track at the first corner, a manoeuvre that secured the championship for Senna.

*Slick rear tyre*

*Radiator air intake*

## ▲MIGHTY STRUGGLE

Michael Schumacher in this Ferrari F310B won the Japanese Grand Prix in 1997 after his championship rival, Jacques Villeneuve, who drove for Williams, was disqualified. The 1997 championship was hotly contested between Schumacher's Ferrari and Villeneuve's Williams up to the final race in Spain, where Villeneuve's third place clinched the title.

## ▶FERRARI'S RIVAL

Victory went to Ayrton Senna's Marlboro McLaren MP4/8 in the 1993 Japanese Grand Prix at Suzuka. This win brought McLaren's total number of victories to 103, equalling the record held by Ferrari.

*Ayrton Senna, McLaren MP4/8*

*Williams*

## ▲WIN FOR MCLAREN

The winner of the 1991 Japanese Grand Prix was Gerhard Berger in his McLaren MP4/6. The car was powered by a 3.5-litre V12 engine developing 780 bhp, and had a carbon-fibre monocoque body. Ayrton Senna, who also drove for McLaren, was second. In the background is the famous Ferris wheel which dominates the Suzuka circuit.

## ▲ RACING IN THE RAIN

Michael Schumacher leads the 1994 Japanese Grand Prix in the Benetton-Ford B194 powered by Ford's Zetec-R V8 engine. Schumacher finished a close second behind Damon Hill's Williams.

## ▼ CHAMPIONSHIP DECIDER

Driving a Williams FW18 powered by a Renault RS88 V10 engine, Damon Hill clinched the 1996 Formula One World Championship with a victory at Suzuka. The win put him 19 points ahead of team-mate Jacques Villeneuve, who lost a wheel from his Williams on lap 37.

On-board television camera

Rear wing to generate downforce

Low-set front wing

## ▲ WASTED EFFORT

Rubens Barrichello drove this Sasol-Jordan in the Japanese Grand Prix in 1994. Powered by a Hart V10 engine, its right rear quarter was rebuilt after Barrichello crashed during practice. However, he then retired with gear-shift problems in the race itself.

McLaren

## ▲ SLIPPERY WHEN WET

Driving this Williams-Renault, Damon Hill lost time in the 1993 Japanese Grand Prix when he hit oil on a corner, having boldly switched to slick tyres on a still-damp track after running on rain tyres. He finished in fourth place, while victory went to Senna's Marlboro McLaren.

## ▲ GOOD CORNERING

Nelson Piquet won the 1990 Japanese Grand Prix in this Benetton B190 with a Ford HBV8 engine. Piquet had set his car's rear wing to give greater downforce to improve cornering around the twisting Suzuka circuit.

### SUZUKA

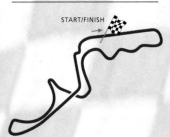

START/FINISH

Built in 1962, the challenging Suzuka circuit at Nagoya is located in an amusement park complete with Ferris wheel. Its crossover loop is a rare feature in Formula One.

# 1990-2000 The Williams Marque

**Williams** AFTER SEVERAL SEASONS as driver and entrant, Frank Williams became a constructor in 1972 with backing from Politoys. However, it was not until 1979 that the marque achieved success, when the FW07 won five Grands Prix. The following year Williams took their first drivers' and constructors' titles and soon became the marque to beat. Driver Keke Rosberg won the last championship with the Ford DFV engine in 1982. The company then turned to Honda for its power units and by late 1985 the Williams-Honda was the Formula One pace-setter. The company continues to be successful despite a car accident in 1986 that confined Frank Williams to a wheelchair.

### ▲ FINAL SEASON

Nigel Mansell drove this Williams-Renault in his final Formula One season in 1992. He finished as champion with a record number of victories, and went on to drive IndyCars.

Rear suspension

Radiator

Water rail

Renault V10 RSI engine

Air intake

Oil feed to engine

### ▲ UP, UP, AND AWAY

David Coulthard's Williams-Renault FW17 RS7 V10 takes to the air in the 1995 Monaco Grand Prix after hitting Jean Alessi's Ferrari 412 T2 at the Ste Devote corner.

Slick racing tyre

Rear wing mainplane

### ▲ DOUBLE CHAMPIONS

Nelson Picquet took second place in the 1987 British Grand Prix in his Williams-Honda FW11B, just behind team-mate Nigel Mansell. Williams went on to win the constructors' championship for the second successive year.

### ▲ WILLIAMS-RENAULT

In 1990, its second year with Renault V10 power, Williams came fourth in the constructors' championship, despite wins at San Marino and Hungary. Team driver Riccardo Patrese started in his 200th Grand Prix at Silverstone that year.

## ► BACK-TO-BACK WINNERS

With backing from Saudi Arabian businessmen, the Williams FW07C of 1981 was developed from the ground-effect FW07B, which had brought Williams the constructors' title the year before. Breeding showed as team driver Alan Jones steered Williams to yet another constructors' championship.

## ▲ WELL-DESERVED VICTORY

There were high hopes that Damon Hill would win the 1996 British Grand Prix in his Williams-Renault. However, a faulty wheel bearing put him out of the race and his team-mate Jacques Villeneuve clinched the victory.

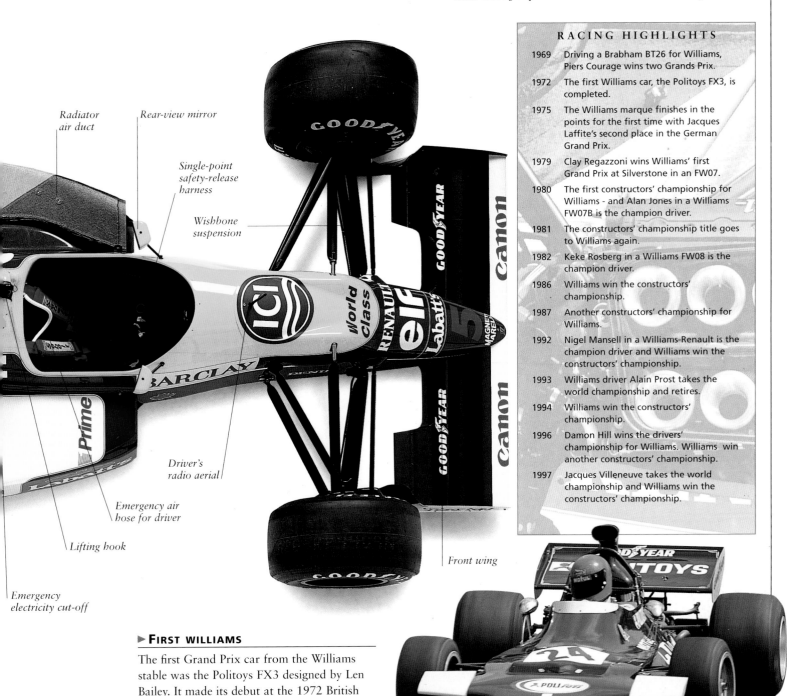

*Radiator air duct*

*Rear-view mirror*

*Single-point safety-release harness*

*Wishbone suspension*

*Driver's radio aerial*

*Emergency air hose for driver*

*Lifting hook*

*Emergency electricity cut-off*

*Front wing*

### RACING HIGHLIGHTS

| | |
|---|---|
| 1969 | Driving a Brabham BT26 for Williams, Piers Courage wins two Grands Prix. |
| 1972 | The first Williams car, the Politoys FX3, is completed. |
| 1975 | The Williams marque finishes in the points for the first time with Jacques Laffite's second place in the German Grand Prix. |
| 1979 | Clay Regazzoni wins Williams' first Grand Prix at Silverstone in an FW07. |
| 1980 | The first constructors' championship for Williams - and Alan Jones in a Williams FW07B is the champion driver. |
| 1981 | The constructors' championship title goes to Williams again. |
| 1982 | Keke Rosberg in a Williams FW08 is the champion driver. |
| 1986 | Williams win the constructors' championship. |
| 1987 | Another constructors' championship for Williams. |
| 1992 | Nigel Mansell in a Williams-Renault is the champion driver and Williams win the constructors' championship. |
| 1993 | Williams driver Alain Prost takes the world championship and retires. |
| 1994 | Williams win the constructors' championship. |
| 1996 | Damon Hill wins the drivers' championship for Williams. Williams win another constructors' championship. |
| 1997 | Jacques Villeneuve takes the world championship and Williams win the constructors' championship. |

## ► FIRST WILLIAMS

The first Grand Prix car from the Williams stable was the Politoys FX3 designed by Len Bailey. It made its debut at the 1972 British Grand Prix, driven by Henri Pescarolo, but was eliminated by an accident.

# NASCAR Racing

**1990-2000**

*GOLDEN JUBILEE LOGO*

THE GOVERNING BODY of stock-car racing, NASCAR – the National Association for Stock Car Racing – was founded in 1948. This exciting sport grew out of racing on the hard-packed sands of Daytona Beach, Florida, and speed events at the dirt oval at Charlotte, North Carolina. Today NASCAR is a national sporting attraction supported by the major manufacturers. Although the engines and chassis are highly developed for racing, the makers take care that the external appearance of the racing cars can easily be identified with the production models in the showrooms, to encourage buyers.

## ▲ MONSTER MILE-EATERS

Competitors in the 1996 Winston Cup Spring Race lap at speeds of 225 kph (140 mph) at the Dover Downs International Raceway. Known as the "Monster Mile", the steeply-banked Dover circuit is on the Delaware peninsula, east of Washington DC.

## ▲ SPEED ON THE STRAIGHTAWAY

Competing in the 1998 June 500 race, Kyle Petty speeds down the straightaway at Pocono International Raceway, Pennsylvania, in his Pontiac Grand Prix.

## ▼ HOLDING OFF A CHALLENGE

The Chevrolet Monte Carlo of Ricky Cravin holds off a challenge from the Ford Thunderbird driven by Bill Elliott at the Rockingham Speedway, North Carolina, a banked circuit which hosts two annual 500-mile (800-km) races.

## ▶ CHEVY CHASER

Terry Labonte is seen here competing in the prestigious Daytona 500 in Florida at the wheel of a Chevy Monte Carlo. Labonte won the NASCAR Winston Cup championship in 1984 and 1996.

## ▼ CHANGE OF LEADERSHIP

The lead changed 15 times during the 1992 Daytona 500, and Davey Allen in this Havoline Ford Thunderbird was the man in front five of those times. Allen duly went on to win the race.

*Manufacturer's logo*

*Rear spoiler*

## ▲ NARROW MARGIN

A narrow victory for Sterling Marlin's Morgan-McClure Kodak Film Chevy Lumina in the 1994 running of NASCAR's flagship race, the Daytona 500. In second place is Ernie Irvan in a Ford Thunderbird.

*Aerodynamic front end*

*Protective netting*

## ▼ WINNING DOUBLE

Dale Jarrett, here driving a 1998 Ford Taurus, is the only driver to have won the NASCAR double of the Daytona 500 and the Indianapolis 400 in the same year, 1996.

*Jeff Burton, Ford T Bird*

## ◄ DOWN IN THE GLEN

Ward Burton in a Pontiac Grand Prix is closely followed by a group of cars around the last of the eleven bends at Watkins Glen, New York State, in the "Bud at the Glen" race, one of the most exciting events on the NASCAR calendar in the mid 1990s.

*Ward Burton, Pontiac Grand Prix*

*Roll cage*

*Hand-built bodywork*

## ► SIBLING RIVALRY

Bobby Labonte, seen here at the wheel of his Chevrolet Monte Carlo, and his brother Terry, two-times winner of the Winston Cup, are the only siblings to have both won championships in major NASCAR race series.

## ▲ IN THE PITS

Here, taking advantage of a yellow caution flag that has slowed the racing, competitors gather nose to tail in the pits at Rockingham Speedway, North Carolina, which has hosted 500-mile (800-km) events since 1965.

# 1990-2000 McLaren Mercedes MP4-13

DESIGNED TO MEET the tough new regulations brought in for 1998 to curb the potential performance of Formula One cars, the McLaren Mercedes MP4-13 incorporated over 12,000 hours of aerodynamic development work in the wind tunnel. It had also to meet stringent new safety standards which had raised crash test loads by up to 50 per cent. The car features a chassis moulded from carbon fibre and aluminium honeycomb composite which incorporates front-, rear-, and side-impact structures and an integral fuel cell. Its all-alloy quad-cam 3-litre V10 "Mercedes-Benz" engine is actually a product of the British company Ilmor and was designed by a team led by Mario Ilien.

## ▲ CHAMPIONSHIP WINNER

Finnish driver Mika Hakkinen won the world championship for McLaren in 1998 in this MP4-13 after a thrilling contest with Michael Schumacher's Ferrari that went to the last race of the season.

## ► LIGHTWEIGHT ENGINE

The McLaren Mercedes MP4-13 is powered by an all-alloy 72-degree V10 engine with two camshafts per bank and four valves per cylinder. Together, the engine and clutch weigh just 107 kg (236 lb).

## ▼ SLEEK AND SAFE

The sleek profile of the 1998 McLaren Mercedes conceals a package of safety measures, including a shock-absorbing hybrid composite structure that is half as strong again as the 1997 model.

*Exhaust system*

*Water and oil pump assembly*

*Rear wing end plate*

*Rear wing elements*

*On-board TV mini-camera*

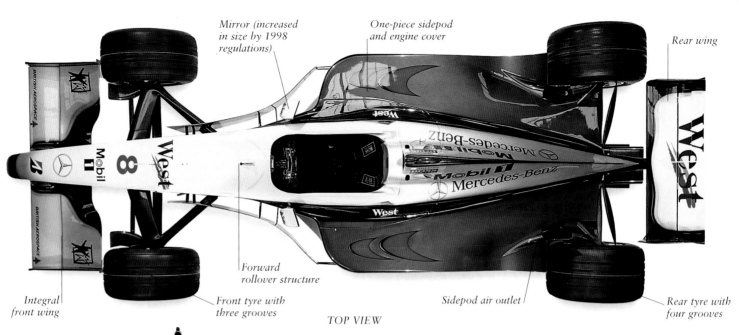

*Mirror (increased in size by 1998 regulations)*

*One-piece sidepod and engine cover*

*Rear wing*

*Integral front wing*

*Forward rollover structure*

*Front tyre with three grooves*

*Sidepod air outlet*

*Rear tyre with four grooves*

TOP VIEW

*Rollover structure combined with engine air intake*

FRONT VIEW

REAR VIEW

## ▲ SHAPED BY THE RULES

New Formula One regulations have shaped the MP4-13. The 1998 rules dictated a slightly longer body, narrower track, minimum chassis width, and the more advanced positioning of the side-impact structure.

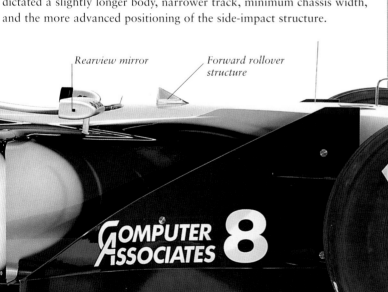

*Rearview mirror*

*Forward rollover structure*

| SPECIFICATION | | Transmission | longitudinal six-speed |
|---|---|---|---|
| | | Power output | 700 bhp |
| Chassis | moulded carbon | Weight | 600 kg (1320 lb) |
| | fibre/aluminium | Suspension | double wishbone with |
| | honeycomb composite | | push-rod inboard torsion |
| Engine | V10 | | bar/damper (front) |
| Valve type | two inlet, two exhaust; | | double wishbone with |
| | two camshafts per bank | | push-rod inboard bell- |
| | | | crank spring/damper |
| | | | (rear) |
| | | Top speed | 350 kph (220 mph) |
| | | Fuel | unleaded petrol |

*Front wing endplate allows adjustment of front wing*

# 1990-2000 The Australian Grand Prix

ALTHOUGH AUSTRALIA had held its first Grand Prix as far back as 1928, it did not host a world championship race until 1985, when the city of Adelaide created a circuit at the centre of its Victoria Park Racecourse. With the backing of South Australia's Premier, a deal was struck with the Formula One Constructors' Association; and the Australian Grand Prix became one of the most popular events in the Formula One calendar. The Adelaide circuit was eventually supplanted by Melbourne but is fondly remembered as one of the best street circuits in motor racing.

*GRANDSTAND AT ADELAIDE*

## ▼ OUT OF CONTENTION

This Ford-powered Dallara was one of the regular backmarkers during the 1990 season. The Adelaide Grand Prix was no exception: both Dallaras retired before quarter distance.

*Jean Alesi (Ferrari)*

*Gerhard Berger (Ferrari)*

*Michael Schumacher (Benetton-Ford)*

*Alain Prost (Williams-Renault)*

## ▲ MARQUE IN DECLINE

The Brabham marque was in terminal decline in 1990 when this V8 Judd-engined BT59 raced at Adelaide. Driver Stefano Modena could only manage 12th place.

## ▲ LEADER OF THE PACK

After two false starts, Ayrton Senna's McLaren MP4/8 leads the pack into the first corner on the Adelaide circuit in the 1993 Australian Grand Prix. Senna won the race and McLaren overtook Ferrari as the most successful Grand Prix team of all time.

## ▼ FAILURE FOR LOTUS

In 1990 Lotus produced this Type 102, powered by a 3.5-litre V12 Lamborghini engine. However, it was not a successful model and withdrew from the 1990 Australian Grand Prix before the halfway mark.

## ▲ CHAMPIONSHIP CLIMAX

Alain Prost leads team-mate Damon Hill, both driving Williams-Renault FW15s, during the 1993 Australian Grand Prix. Prost went on to become that season's world champion driver.

### ADELAIDE

START/FINISH

While Adelaide is basically a street circuit, it is still very fast, with a testing sequence of sharp right-hand bends and a long straight where, in the 1980s, the Grand Prix cars could reach maximum speed. It was supplanted by Melbourne in 1995.

## ◄ KNOCKED OUT

This V10 Williams FW16B-Renault was driven by Damon Hill at Adelaide in 1994. Hill lost the championship by a single point after being involved in a collision during this race.

## ► SURVIVING THE CRASH

Martin Brundle survived his Jordan-Peugeot breaking in half after spinning and colliding with Johnny Herbert's Sauber-Ford in the 1996 Melbourne Grand Prix.

*Damon Hill (Williams-Renault)*

## ▼ CHAMPIONSHIP WINNER

Michael Schumacher drove this Benetton in the 1994 Adelaide Grand Prix. Powered by a Ford Zetec-R V8 engine, the car gained the 1994 world championship for Schumacher.

*Ayrton Senna (McLaren-Ford)*

139

# RACING PERSONALITIES 3

Motor racing is a story of people as well as machines, for without the great drivers, engineers, and team managers, the cars would be nothing. Mechanical superiority is of no value without the skills that maximize its potential, whether it be unmatched ability at the wheel or the propensity to spot a loophole in technical regulations and design a car that can drive right through them! The personalities included here are some of the very greatest names in motor racing; people fired with the common ambition to go further and faster than their rivals, whose extraordinary abilities have made them household names. Yet despite their boundless desire to triumph, these people have always simply been, as one motoring authority commented, "guys who just love to be around cars". Their aspirations and dreams remain constant and that is what makes motor racing so special.

## A

### MARIO ANDRETTI
### 1940–

Mario Andretti, who was born in Italy but took American citizenship, chose motor racing as a career after being inspired by the 1954 Monza Grand Prix. Five years later, Andretti emigrated to the United States where he entered stock-car races. It was not long before he had graduated to the USAC big car championship races,

*MARIO ANDRETTI*

where he became one of the most successful drivers of his generation. By 1968 he was racing in Formula One and over the next 14 years he entered 128 Grands Prix and won 12 of them. He reached his pinnacle in 1978 when he became Formula One World Champion. Andretti also won a variety of other races, including the Indianapolis 500, four IndyCar championships, and the Daytona 500 NASCAR race.

*ALBERTO ASCARI*

### ANTONIO AND
### ALBERTO ASCARI
### 1888–1925 AND 1918–1955

The Italian Antonio Ascari achieved his first racing successes in 1919 with a modified 1914 Grand Prix Fiat. Soon afterwards he took on an Alfa Romeo agency and inspired the creation of the Tipo ES 20/30 sports car. He graduated to Grand Prix racing at the wheel of the Alfa Romeo P2 Grand Prix car, winning the 1924 Italian and 1925 Belgian Grands Prix, before crashing fatally while leading the 1925 French Grand Prix at Montlhéry. Antonio Ascari's son, Alberto, began racing motorbikes and was offered his first car drive in the 1940 Mille Miglia. In 1946 he gained a place in the Maserati works-backed Scuderia Ambrosiana, his first victory coming in the 1947 Circuit of Modena. In 1949 he joined Ferrari and won 33 Formula One and Formula Two Grands Prix. He was world champion in 1952 and 1953. He also won the 1954 Mille Miglia. Ascari was killed testing a Ferrari at Monza, 30 years to the day after his father's death.

## B

### WOOLF BARNATO
### 1895–1948

The son of a British diamond millionaire, "Babe" Barnato inherited most of his father's wealth at the age of two, and, at the age of 25, began to race at Brooklands with an 8-litre Locomobile. He bought his first Bentley in 1925 and was soon persuaded to back the Bentley company with £100,000. In return he was given a place in the works racing team. An outstanding driver, Barnato won three Le Mans races in a row for Bentley.

### DEREK BELL
### 1941–

Derek Bell is one of Britain's most successful endurance racers. He first won Le Mans in 1975 in a Gulf-Mirage GR8, with Jackie Ickx as co-driver. The same pair won again in 1981 driving a Porsche 936, and in 1982 with a Porsche 956. Bell achieved two more Le Mans victories in 1986 and 1987, each time driving a Porsche 926C.

*DEREK BELL*

### BHANUBAN BIRABONGSE
### 1914–1985

The Thai Prince Bhanuban Birabongse raced under the name of B. Bira, beginning at the age of 20 with a Riley Imp in 1935. For his 21st birthday, in July 1935, his cousin and racing manager Prince Chula bought him one of the new 1500cc ERAs. In this car Bira gained ten firsts, eight seconds, and five thirds from 1935 to 1939. Bira also raced Delage and Maserati cars. After World War II he returned to racing with Maseratis, before finally retiring in 1955.

### SIR HENRY BIRKIN
### 1896–1933

In 1921 British racer Sir Henry "Tim" Birkin began racing at Brooklands with a wooden-bodied DFP as a respite from office work. Business pressures then compelled him to retire from the track until 1927, when he and his brother Archie raced a 3-litre Bentley. Birkin became a full-time racing driver soon after. With Jean Chassagne as co-driver, he finished fifth in the 1927 Le Mans with a works 4.5-litre Bentley. Birkin then received backing to set up his own factory at Welwyn in Hertfordshire. He already had plans to build supercharged versions of the 4.5-litre Bentley. After Bentley were taken over by Rolls-Royce, Birkin raced Bugattis, Alfa Romeos, and Maseratis. He died from septicaemia as a result of burning his arm on the exhaust pipe of his car during practice for the 1933 Tripoli Grand Prix.

*SIR HENRY BIRKIN*

## GEORGES BOILLOT
### 1885–1916

Peugeot driver Georges Boillot began racing Lion-Peugeot voiturettes in 1908 and gained his first victory at Caen the following year. With designer Ernest Henry, the Frenchman Boillot was part of a special racing department at Peugeot, responsible for the first twin-cam racing engine. This powered the 1912 Grand Prix Peugeot which Boillot drove to victory in that year's French Grand Prix. In 1913 he won both the Coupe de l'Auto and the Grand Prix in 3-litre and 5.7-litre twin-cam Peugeots. However, the superior performance of the German Mercedes team forced him to retire from the 1914 Grand Prix at Lyons. Boillot died in aerial combat in World War I.

*GEORGES BOILLOT*

## PIETRO BORDINO
### 1890–1928

The Italian Pietro Bordino became a works Fiat driver at the age of 18. He raced at Brooklands in 1913 with a 28.3-litre 300-hp Fiat, reputedly capable of 290 kph (180 mph), but his postwar career was often marred by mechanical failures when victory seemed within his grasp. However, in 1922, he won the Voiturette Grand Prix and the 2-litre Grand Prix in the inaugural meeting at Monza. Bordino switched to Bugatti for 1928 when Fiat withdrew from racing. He was drowned during the Circuit of Alessandria when his T35 Bugatti hit a stray dog and plunged into a river which ran beside the track.

## SIR JACK BRABHAM
### 1926–

Born in Australia, Jack Brabham emigrated to England in 1955 and opted to race for Cooper. Success was not far away; in 1959 and 1960 he won the world championships. In 1961 he left Cooper to establish his own Grand Prix team. The new Brabham-Climax BT3 made its Formula One debut the following year. The first Brabham victory came three years later at the 1964 French Grand Prix. Brabham persuaded Australian components company Repco to develop a 3-litre version of their Tasman Series V8 engine. Brabham won the 1966 French Grand Prix with the new Brabham-Repco, making him the first driver to win in a car bearing his own name. He retired from racing in 1970 and was knighted in 1984.

## TONY BROOKS
### 1932–

Britain's Tony Brooks made his Formula Two debut at Crystal Palace in August 1955 at the wheel of a Connaught. He finished fourth, behind three Formula One cars. In his first drive in Formula One, he won the 1955 Syracuse Grand Prix, Sicily, in a Connaught, the first win by a British car since 1924.

*TONY BROOKS*

He drove for the ill-starred BRM team in 1956, and moved to Vanwall in 1958, winning the Belgian, German, and Italian Grands Prix. He also co-drove with Stirling Moss the Aston Martin that won the 1958 RAC Tourist Trophy. He moved to Ferrari in 1959 and was runner-up in the world championship. Brooks retired in 1961.

*JACK BRABHAM*

*ETTORE BUGATTI*

## ETTORE BUGATTI
### 1881–1947

Ettore Bugatti, the son of Italian artist and furniture designer Carlo Bugatti, designed his first car – a 3054cc four-cylinder machine – at the age of 20. After a period working with firms in Alsace, Strasbourg, and Cologne, Bugatti set up on his own account in 1910 at Molsheim, back in Alsace. The marque's first major victory came in 1920 at the Voiturette Grand Prix, Le Mans, with a prewar 16-valve T13. The 1924 T35 straight-eight overhead-cam Grand Prix Bugatti dominated Grand Prix racing for much of the 1920s, and its T51 dohc derivative of 1931 continued the trend until the arrival of the new Alfa Romeos and Maseratis in 1934. By the mid-1930s the cost of Grand Prix racing had become far too onerous for Bugatti's little company, and focus was transferred to the design and production of sports cars. The move was successful; the T57G "Tank" won the 1936 French sports car Grand Prix and the 1937 and 1938 Le Mans 24-hour events.

## C

### ALESSANDRO CAGNO
### 1883–1970

An undemonstrative driver, the Italian Cagno drove for Fiat between 1901 and 1906, taking third place in the 1905 Gordon Bennett race. He then joined Itala, winning the Targa Florio in 1906 and the Coppa della Velocità in 1907. In 1908 he took up flying, but he made a spectacular racing comeback in 1923 with a 1.5-litre Fiat, gaining the first-ever victory for a supercharged car in the Italian Voiturette Grand Prix.

### GIUSEPPE CAMPARI
### 1892–1933

The 16-stone Italian Campari was an unlikely-looking racing driver with a passion for opera. Driving for Alfa Romeo, he achieved his first victory on the Mugello Circuit in 1920. He won the 1924 French Grand Prix in the new Alfa Romeo P2 and was leading the 1925 French Grand Prix when the Alfa Romeo team retired after Ascari's fatal crash. He won the 1928 and 1929 Mille Miglia and Coppa Acerbo races and was second in the 1931 Mille Miglia in an Alfa Romeo 6C1750. In 1933 he won the French Grand Prix and announced that he would retire after his next race, the Monza Grand Prix, to devote himself to opera. However, his car skidded in the second heat and he was killed.

## SIR MALCOLM CAMPBELL
### 1885–1949

The most famous member of the English Campbell family, Malcolm won his first race in 1910 in a Darracq. After World War I he raced a variety of cars, including a 1912 7.6-litre Grand Prix Peugeot and the 350-hp V12 Sunbeam, with which he set a new land speed record of 235.2 kph (146.16 mph) in 1924. From then on he combined track racing with attempts on the Land Speed Record driving his aeroengined Bluebirds. It was his land speed records that won him a knighthood in 1931 when he reached 395.7 kph (246 mph). In 1935 he broke the 300-mph (482.8 kph) barrier at Bonneville salt flats in Utah, USA.

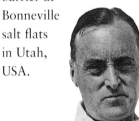

*SIR MALCOLM CAMPBELL*

## RUDI CARACCIOLA
### 1901–1959

Rudi Caracciola from Germany started racing in 1922 with a Fafnir light car and joined the Mercedes team in 1924, driving a 1.5-litre supercharged Mercedes. His first major victory was the 1926 German Grand Prix, and he also won the inaugural race at the new Nürburgring circuit that year. When Mercedes withdrew from racing at the end of 1931, Caracciola joined Alfa Romeo, winning four Grands Prix during 1932, but he crashed at Monaco in 1933, breaking his thigh badly. Out of action for over a year, he rejoined Mercedes who had a new government-sponsored Grand Prix car. He co-drove the winning Mercedes in the 1934 Italian Grand Prix and took eight Grand Prix victories the following year to become German and European champion. With the new W154 Mercedes, he won the 1938 Swiss Grand Prix and Coppa Acerbo, and his last victory was in the 1939 German Grand Prix.

### COLIN CHAPMAN
### 1928–1982

One of the great British innovators of motor-racing history, Chapman built his first Austin Seven-based Lotus between 1947 and 1948, and formed Lotus Engineering in 1952. Lotus made its Formula One debut with a Type 12 in the 1958 Monaco Grand Prix. When Formula One looked doomed for want of a suitable 3-litre engine in 1966,

*COLIN CHAPMAN*

Chapman persuaded the Ford company to commission a new V8 Formula One engine from Cosworth. The new Lotus-Ford 49, driven by Jim Clark, won first time out in 1967. Distraught by Clark's death in 1968, Chapman almost pulled out of motor racing. However, he stayed, and his dynamism and imagination kept Lotus at the top of Formula One racing during the 1970s.

## LOUIS CHEVROLET
### 1878–1941

The son of a Swiss watch-maker, Louis Chevrolet worked in the French motor industry before emigrating to Canada in 1900. By 1905 he was working for Hol-Tan (Hollander & Tangeman) in New York, and set a new mile record driving a Fiat racing car. Chevrolet then joined the Buick racing team and became one of America's leading racing drivers. He founded the Frontenac Motor Company to build racing cars, and also designed the monocoque-bodied Cornelian light racer. Chevrolet decided to give up racing after the death of his brother Gaston in a crash at a board-track event in California, USA.

## LUIGI CHINETTI
### 1906–1980

Italian-born Luigi Chinetti won Le Mans in 1932 and 1934 driving 8C Alfa Romeos and emigrated to the United States shortly before World War II. In 1946 he visited Italy and persuaded his friend Enzo Ferrari to build racing cars; he became the American agent for the new Ferrari marque. He won Le Mans again in 1949, driving the Ferrari 166.

## LOUIS CHIRON
### 1900–1979

Born in Monaco, Louis Chiron began racing a Bugatti in 1923, and by 1928 he had become one of Europe's leading drivers, winning five Grands Prix that season. He finished seventh in 1929 at Indianapolis, the year in which he helped to create the Monaco Grand Prix. He drove for Alfa Romeo in the early 1930s, and won the 1934 French Grand Prix at Montlhéry. His career waned after that, though he won the French Grands Prix of 1947 and 1948 with Talbots. He also won the 1954 Monte Carlo Rally in a Lancia.

*LOUIS CHIRON*

## JIM CLARK
### 1936–1968

Driving in local rallies brought Scottish farmer's son Jim Clark to fame in the world of motor sport in the early 1950s. His run of success really began in 1960 when he took third place at Le Mans for Aston Martin and was also recruited to drive for Lotus. A natural winner from the start of his career, Clark was soon being entered in Grands Prix. His first Grand Prix victory came at Spa, Belgium, in 1962 with the new monocoque Lotus 25. He would have won the world championship had his car not sprung an oil leak while he was in the lead during the final race in South Africa. Clark took the championship in 1963, however, winning six races. The following year he lost it by the narrowest of margins in the last race of the season. In 1965, he again won the world championship as well as scoring a resounding victory in the Indy 500 with his Lotus-Ford. He was less successful in 1966, with Lotus forced to use the troublesome H16 BRM engine. However, 1967 saw a historic event when he drove the new Ford DFV-engined Lotus 49 to a first-time victory in the Dutch Grand Prix. Clark went on to win his 25th Grand Prix at the beginning of 1968 but was killed soon afterwards in a crash during a Formula Two race at Hockenheim.

*JIM CLARK*

## JOHN COBB
### 1899–1952

British driver John Cobb won his first race at Brooklands in 1925 with a 10-litre Fiat. In 1929 he acquired the 10.5-litre V12 Delage, which had set a world speed record of 230.6 kph (143.3 mph) in 1924 and 11 British records, lapping Brooklands at over 200 kph (125 mph). In 1933 Cobb unveiled his Napier-Railton, designed by Reid Railton. In 1935, powered by a 24-litre

*JOHN COBB*

W12 Napier Lion aviation engine, it achieved the fastest speed recorded at the track, almost 244 kph (152 mph). In 1939 Cobb set a new land speed record of 594.9 kph (369.7 mph) in the Railton Mobil Special, powered by two 1250 bhp Napier aeroengines, one driving the front wheels, the other the rear. Cobb was killed when his jet boat *Crusader* exploded while attempting to break the water speed record in 1952.

### PETER COLLINS
### 1931–1958

England's Peter Collins started in 500cc racing at the age of 17 and was driving for HWM's Formula Two team within three years. In 1952 he was racing sports cars for Aston Martin and won the 1952 Goodwood Nine-Hours race and the 1953 Ulster Tourist Trophy. In 1954 he started Grand Prix racing, driving the Ferrari Thin Wall Special for Tony Vandervell's new Grand Prix team. He joined Ferrari in 1956, winning two Grands Prix with the Lancia-Ferrari. For 1957 he was joined at Ferrari by his friend Mike Hawthorn, but he

enjoyed only modest success until new cars came along in 1958, when he won the British Grand Prix at Silverstone. However, in the next race, the German Grand Prix, Collins was fatally injured in a crash.

### CHARLES AND JOHN COOPER
### 1893–1964 AND 1923–

English garage owner Charles Cooper and his son John were among the first to build cars for the new 500cc Formula. In 1952 Cooper began building Bristol-engined cars for the 2-litre Formula Two, and rising star Mike Hawthorn won two races at Goodwood in the new model. In 1958 Cooper produced a 2-litre Formula One racer based on the previous year's successful 1500cc Coventry-Climax-powered Formula Two car. The car was an instant winner; Stirling Moss secured Cooper's first Formula One win in the Argentine Grand Prix. In 1959, with the engine uprated to 2.5-litres, Cooper took the constructors' championship, with Jack Brabham taking the drivers' title; both driver and constructor repeated the feat in 1960.

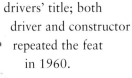

*PETER COLLINS*

### EARL COOPER
### 1886–1965

The American Earl Cooper took up motor racing in his early twenties and spent several years competing on the California dirt tracks. His big break came in 1913 when he was invited to join the Stutz racing team and won the American Automobile Association's National Championship. Stutz had little success in 1914, when Cooper retired during his first attempt at the Indianapolis 500, so Harry Stutz copied the top European racing engines from Peugeot and Delage. Three cars were built and painted white. Cooper was immediately successful with his "White Squadron" car, winning the National Championship for the second time. Stutz gave up racing in 1916 so Cooper bought one of the White Squadron cars and won the National Championship for the third time in 1917. He retired from racing in 1921.

### BRIGGS CUNNINGHAM
### 1907–

American Briggs Cunningham formed the B.S. Cunningham Company in 1950 to build the V8-engined Cunningham sports car. In 1951 three Cunningham C2-Rs raced at Le Mans, though only one completed the race. In 1952 a Cunningham C4-R took fourth place at Le Mans, while in the 1953 race three Cunninghams were among the first 10. In 1954, Cunningham C4-Rs finished third and fifth at Le Mans. Thereafter, production of Cunninghams ceased.

## D

### S.C.H. DAVIS
### 1887–1981

Englishman S.C.H. "Sammy" Davis began as a Daimler apprentice before becoming a motor sport journalist and illustrator. Davis also raced, and in 1922 he was part of the Aston Martin team which smashed 32 world and class records at Brooklands. He competed in the Le Mans endurance race in 1926 and 1927, winning the later race after extricating his 3-litre Bentley from a multi-car pile-up at White House Corner. In 1930 Davis and the Earl of March won the Brooklands 500-mile (800-km) race in an Austin Seven driven at 134.26 kph (83.41 mph).

### KAYE DON
### 1891–1981

Briton Kaye Don achieved fame at Brooklands in the 1920s with his 12-litre Hispano aeroengined Viper, and in 1928 he became the first man to lap the Brooklands outer circuit at over 200 kph (130 mph), with the V12

*KAYE DON*

Sunbeam Tiger. He also won the Ulster Tourist Trophy that year in a Lea-Francis. In 1931 he set a new Brooklands lap record of 221.37 kph (137.58 mph). Don retired in 1934 after the death of his mechanic in a crash on the Isle of Man which led to his conviction for manslaughter.

## KEITH DUCKWORTH
### 1933–

Designer of the most successful Grand Prix engine of all time, Briton Keith Duckworth founded Cosworth Engineering (with Mike Costin) in 1958 after a spell as transmission engineer with Lotus. In 1965 Ford put up the £100,000 development costs of the Duckworth V8 Cosworth DFV Grand Prix engine. The first-time-out victory for Jim Clark's Lotus 49 in the 1967 Dutch Grand Prix was the first of an unrivalled string of 155 Formula One victories for the DFV. A short-stroke version of the DFV, the 2.65-litre DFX, won ten Indianapolis 500s.

## E

## BERNIE ECCLESTONE
### 1930–

One-time motorbike racer and dealer, Englishman Bernie Ecclestone started racing in Formula Three in the 1950s. An early venture into team management with a couple of Connaughts driven by Ivor Bueb and Stuart Lewis-Evans ended with Lewis-Evans' death in 1958. In 1971 Ecclestone took over Motor Racing Developments (which ran the Brabham team) and set up the

Formula One Constructors' Association. This became the mouthpiece for Grand Prix racing and made Ecclestone the most powerful man in motor sport, with control over the sport's television rights.

## S.F. EDGE
### 1868–1940

Australian-born Selwyn Francis Edge realized the value of motor sport success as a sales tool when he founded the Motor Power Company to sell the new Napier car. He won Britain's first major victory in a Continental race in 1902 when his Napier outlasted the opposition in the Gordon Bennett contest. His career as a race driver ended after 1904, but in 1907 he established a world 24-hour record of 105.1 kph (65.91 mph) in a six-cylinder Napier at the new Brooklands track. The record stood until he broke it in 1922 with a six-cylinder Spyker car which averaged 119.68 kph (74.27 mph) at Brooklands.

*S.F. EDGE*

## JUAN MANUEL FANGIO
### 1911–1995

A world champion five times over, and possibly the greatest driver of all time, Juan Manuel Fangio won 24 Grands Prix from only 51 starts. A first generation Argentinian of Italian descent, he started racing in the 1930s. When racing restarted in Argentina after World War II, Fangio was chosen to drive one of two Maseratis acquired by the Argentine Automobile Club to match the visiting European

drivers. In 1949 he went to Europe, and was snapped up by Alfa Romeo to join their team for the first world championship in 1950. He won his first championship in 1951, then moved to Ferrari, but a broken neck kept him out of racing until 1953. Back with Maserati, he was runner-up that year, then joined Mercedes and won the next two world championships. He rejoined Ferrari for 1956 and again won the championship. In 1957, he won his last world championship – this time for Maserati – and retired in 1958.

## GUISEPPE FARINA
### 1906–1966

Italian Guiseppe "Nino" Farina was a member of the famous Turin coachbuilding family. He started driving at the age of 15 and won his first major race, the Masaryk Voiturette Grand Prix, Brno, in a Maserati in 1934. In 1936, he joined the Scuderia Ferrari, where he raced against the might of the

*FROM LEFT TO RIGHT: ALBERTO ASCARI, JUAN FANGIO, AND GUISEPPE FARINA*

German teams in generally outmoded Alfa Romeos. He managed second place in the 1939 Swiss Grand Prix with a 1.5-litre Alfetta against ten Mercedes and Auto Unions of double the capacity. In 1950, he won the first of the modern series of world championships for Alfa Romeo. He went to Ferrari in 1952 and became team leader in 1954, but racing injuries he sustained that season eventually forced his retirement in 1957.

### ENZO FERRARI
### 1898–1988

After some success as a driver in the early 1920s, the Italian Enzo Ferrari established his Scuderia Ferrari racing team at the end of 1929, representing the interests of Alfa Romeo. The arrangement was ended in 1938 and the Ferrari car manufacturing company began in 1947. The new V12 sports racer, designed by Giaocchino Colombo, made its competition debut at Piacenza that May; the first Grand Prix single-seater appeared the

*ENZO FERRARI*

following year. In 1961, Ferrari won their first constructors' championship, and won again in 1964, 1975, 1976, 1977, 1979, 1982, and 1983. Ferrari

also won multiple victories in the Mille Miglia and Le Mans. After his only legitimate son, Dino, died in 1956, Enzo Ferrari became a detached, almost reclusive figure, ruling his company from its headquarters at Maranello without watching his cars compete. He rejected a takeover bid from Ford in 1963 only days before the contracts were due to be signed, but his company was subsumed into the Fiat empire six years later. However, Ferrari ran the firm until he died at the age of 90.

### EMERSON FITTIPALDI
### 1946–

Emerson Fittipaldi arrived in Britain in 1969, having already won the kart and Formula Vee

*EMERSON FITTIPALDI*

titles in his native Brazil. Racing school proprietor Jim Russell offered him a drive in his Formula Three Lotus 59, and he won the Lombard Formula Three championship in his debut year. He was signed for Formula Two by Colin Chapman, and was quickly upgraded to Formula One to keep him out of the hands of rival teams. He won his fifth Formula One race, the

US Grand Prix at Watkins Glen, and took the 1972 title for Lotus, becoming the youngest man to win the title. Fittipaldi was runner-up in 1973 before moving to McLaren and taking the 1974 championship. In 1981 he moved to the USA and IndyCar racing, where he became champion in 1986. Fittipaldi won the Indy 500 in 1989, becoming the first driver to win a $1 million-plus purse.

### MAURO FORGHIERI
### c.1936–

For over 20 years this Italian designer was responsible for Ferrari's racing cars. He joined the company in 1959 and contributed to seven world constructors' championship titles, starting with John Surtees' 1964 victory. Forghieri saw his 3-litre V12 power unit overshadowed by the brilliant Ford-Cosworth DFV in the late 1960s, but his 312B1 flat-12 brought hope in the early 1970s. However, successive developments of this design failed to deliver, until the revised 312B3 gave Niki Lauda nine pole positions in 1974. Forghieri's brilliant transverse-gearbox 312T brought Lauda the 1975 championship, and

*MAURO FORGHIERI*

developments of this design won the 1975 and 1977 world titles for Lauda and the 1979 title for Jody Scheckter.

### FROILAN GONZALES
### 1922–

The flamboyant Argentinian driver Froilan Gonzales followed Juan Fangio to Europe in 1950, succeeding him as driver of an Argentine Automobile Club Maserati. Gonzales joined Ferrari the following year, and gave the Italian company its first world championship victory with his win in the British Grand Prix. He raced for Maserati in Formula Two in 1952 and 1953, and won Le Mans in

*FROILAN GONZALES*

1954 with Maurice Trintignant in a 4.9-litre Ferrari. A crash in practice for the 1954 Ulster Tourist Trophy ended his racing career.

### SIR ALGERNON AND KENELM LEE GUINNESS
### 1883–1954 AND 1887–1937

Irishman Sir Algernon "Algy" Lee Guinness came third in the 1905 Isle of Man Tourist Trophy with a Darracq and raced a 200hp V8 Darracq at Brooklands and Saltburn Sands in 1907 and 1908. He later became Vice Chairman of the RAC racing committee. His brother, Kenelm won the 1914 Isle of Man Tourist Trophy with a Sunbeam. After World

*ALGY LEE GUINNESS*

War I, he rejoined the Sunbeam team. He enjoyed his greatest successes, however, with the 1.5-litre Talbot-Darracq voiturettes, coming second in the 1921 Voiturette Grand Prix at Le Mans. In the 1922 Junior Car Club 200-mile (320-km) race at Brooklands, the Talbot-Darracqs faced stiff competion, but Guinness won at an average speed of 141.61 kph

(88.06 mph). In 1922 he set a new land speed record of 215.19 kph (133.75 mph) with the 350-hp V12 Sunbeam at Brooklands, the last time the record was ever broken on a race circuit.

### DAN GURNEY
### 1931–

Dan Gurney came to Europe from America in 1958 to race Ferrari sports cars and was given his first Formula One drive the following season. In 1961 he joined Porsche and gave the marque its only Formula One victory, in the 1962 French Grand Prix. He and Carroll Shelby founded the All-American Racers in 1964, and Gurney took over sole ownership of the company in 1967. His win at the 1967 Belgian Grand Prix in his Formula One Eagle was the first for an American driver in an American car since 1921. Gurney was a highly successful stock-car racer in the 1960s, and co-drove the winning Ford at Le Mans in 1967.

### RAY HARROUN
### 1879–1968

American engineer Ray Harroun had officially retired from racing when his boss Howard Marmon persuaded him to make a "farewell appearance" in the first Indianapolis 500 in 1911. Harroun decided he could do without a riding mechanic, and created the first racing single-seater, the Marmon Wasp. He

*MIKE HAWTHORN*

drove a steady race to defeat cars of far greater engine capacity, and then went back into racing retirement.

### MIKE HAWTHORN
### 1929–1959

Britain's first world champion driver, Mike Hawthorn started racing a Riley Imp in 1950 at the age of 21. He moved into single-seater racing in 1952 with a Cooper-Bristol, then joined Ferrari in 1953 and won the French Grand Prix; he was the first Briton to win that event since 1923. He drove for Vanwall in the early part of 1955 but the car was not fully developed, so he went back to Ferrari. Hawthorn drove a Jaguar D-Type to victory in that year's Le Mans 24-hour race, and raced in Formula One with the new 2.5-litre BRM during 1956. Back with Ferrari, he won the 1958 world championship, and announced his retirement at the end of the season. He was killed in a car crash in January 1959, aged just 29.

### ROBIN HERD
### 1939–

In 1968 English aircraft engineer Robin Herd formed March Engineering with Max Mosley, Graham Coaker, and

Alan Rees. He designed the March 701, which, driven by Chris Amon won first time out at Silverstone in the International Trophy. Herd followed this with the March 711, which March works driver Ronnie Peterson drove to second place in the world championship in 1969. March's first Formula One victory came in 1975 when Vittorio Brambilla won the Austrian Grand Prix. Two years later March effectively pulled out of Formula One, running in only a few races during the 1980s.

### DAMON HILL
### 1960–

The first "second generation" world champion, Britain's Damon Hill was only 15 when his father, Graham, was killed, but had already shown an aptitude for motorcycle trials.

*DAMON HILL*

*GRAHAM HILL*

### DENNY HULME
### 1936–1992

Dennis Clive Hulme left New Zealand in 1960 under the "Driver to Europe" scheme to race in European Formula Junior events. He came second to Jack Brabham in the 1964 Formula Two series and then graduated to Formula One the following year. His first Formula One victory came at Monaco in 1967, and he took the world championship that year. From 1968 until he retired in 1975, he raced for his compatriot Bruce McLaren.

### JAMES HUNT
### 1947–1993

Englishman James Hunt started driving in Formula Three in 1969 and was signed by team patron Lord Hesketh to drive in Formula Two in 1972. When Hunt crashed the Formula Two Surtees that Hesketh had bought for the 1973 season, Lord Hesketh decided to compete in Formula One, initially with a March and then with the Hesketh 308. Hunt managed fourth in the French and British Grands Prix and second at Watkins Glen in his first season. He

In 1984, at the age of 24, Hill tried Formula Ford, and three years later came third. His chance at Formula One came in 1992, and he proved an able test driver for Williams before being signed for 1993 along with Alain Prost. Wins in Hungary, Belgium, and Italy gave him third place in the championship. He won second place in the 1994 and 1995 championships, followed by the world title in 1996. However, Williams failed to renew his contract for 1997, and Hill was forced to race with the less competitive Arrows and Jordan teams during the next two seasons.

### GRAHAM HILL
### 1929–1975

A late starter, Britain's Graham Hill tried a racing car for the first time at the age of 24. He then met Colin Chapman at Brands Hatch, who employed him as a mechanic at the Lotus factory. Hill made his Grand Prix debut in 1958, and joined BRM for 1960, winning their first world championship in 1962. He was runner-up in 1963, 1964, and 1965, and

won Indianapolis in 1966 driving a Lola. He rejoined Lotus in 1967 as team-mate to Jim Clark and won his second championship the following year. He broke both legs in a crash at Watkins Glen in 1969 and, though he won the 1972 Le Mans 24-hour race for Matra, his Formula One edge was gone. He was killed when his aeroplane crashed in thick fog near Elstree Aerodrome, Hertfordshire.

### PHIL HILL
### 1927–

Already a successful sports car racer in his native United States, Phil Hill raced at Le Mans in 1954 before being signed for a series of European

*PHIL HILL*

races by Enzo Ferrari. He was promoted to the factory's Formula One team in 1958, and two years later won his first Grand Prix at Monza. Hill took the world championship in 1961 driving a "sharknose" Ferrari. He retired in 1967.

### LORD HOWE
### (FRANCIS CURZON)
### 1884–1964

Francis Richard Penn Curzon, England's 5th Earl Howe, did not begin his competitive motoring career until the age of 44. His first major event was the 1928 Ulster Tourist Trophy, and he raced again in Ulster in 1930 in a Mercedes 38-250 hp. In 1931 he won Le Mans in his new 8C2300 Alfa Romeo four-seater, with Sir Henry Birkin as co-driver. Together they set a new average speed and distance records of 125.6 kph (78.13 mph) and 3,017 km (1,875 miles). Howe served as British Racing Drivers' Club president from its very first annual general meeting in 1929 until his death in 1964; he was also vice-president of the CSI, forerunner of the FIA.

*JAMES HUNT*

moved to McLaren in 1976 and won the world title with a memorable third place during a rainstorm in Japan. Hunt retired in 1979 and became an accomplished television race commentator before his untimely death from a heart attack in 1993.

## I

### JACKIE ICKX
### 1945–

Belgian-born Jackie Ickx raced saloon cars from 1965 with great success. He was spotted by team boss Ken Tyrrell and signed for Formula Three, progressing to Formula Two in 1966. He was signed for the Ferrari Formula One team in 1968, and came fourth in the championship, then moved to Brabham in 1969, finishing second in the championship. That same year he won Ford's fourth victory at Le Mans in a GT40 #1075. His total of six wins at Le Mans is a record, and he has also won two sports car championships in 1982 and 1983 and the Paris–Dakar Rally.

*JACKIE ICKX*

## J

### CHARLES JARROTT
### 1877–1944

Englishman Charles Jarrott was a racing cyclist in the 1890s. He gravitated into the motor industry and raced motor tricycles before turning to racing Panhard-Levassor cars. He finished tenth in the 1901 Paris–Berlin Race, came second in the 1902 Circuit du Nord, and finished 11th in that year's Paris–Vienna marathon.

*CHARLES JARROTT*

Switching to De Dietrich, he came third in the notorious 1903 Paris–Madrid "Race to Death", moved to Napier for the 1903 Gordon Bennett, and raced Wolseley and De Dietrich cars in 1904, retiring from racing the following year.

### CAMILLE JENATZY
### 1868–1913

The Belgian Camille Jenatzy, known as the "Red Devil", was one of the most dramatic racing drivers of the pre-1910 era. He set the first land speed record to exceed 100 kph (60 mph) in his electric racer,

*CAMILLE JENATZY*

*Jamais Contente*, in 1899. By 1903 he was driving for Mercedes, finishing 11th in class in the Paris–Madrid race. He won the Irish Gordon Bennett race in 1903 at the wheel of a borrowed 60-hp Mercedes after the works entry of 90-hp cars had been destroyed in a fire at the factory. He won the race again in 1904. Jenatzy died in a hunting accident; he was mistakenly shot after imitating the call of a wild boar.

### EDDIE JORDAN
### 1948–

Irish banker Eddie Jordan abandoned a promising career as a racing driver to establish his own Formula Three team in 1981. Jordan won the Formula Three constructors' championship with driver Johnnie Herbert in 1987. The company entered Formula One in 1991. Jordan's first Formula One cars used Ford HB engines, but a 1992 deal to use the new Yamaha V12 proved a disaster. For 1993 Jordan adopted the new Hart V10 power unit, and then made a three-year engine deal with Peugeot. It was Eddie Jordan who "discovered" the champion driver Michael

Schumacher, who won his first Grand Prix in a Jordan before joining Benetton.

## K

### UKYO KATAYAMA
### 1963–

Katayama began racing in Formula Ford in his native country, Japan. He progressed to Formula Three and came to Europe to race in the French Formula Renault series before returning to Formula Three. Back in Japan, he raced in the Japan Formula One 3000 and became the national champion in a Lola Mugen Honda in 1991. Katayama's first Formula One race was the 1992 South African Grand Prix in his Venturi Larrousse-Lamborghini. He moved to Tyrrell in 1993.

## L

### NIKI LAUDA
### 1949–

Austrian Niki Lauda began circuit racing with Formula Vee and Formula Three cars, and then gained a place in the March Formula Two team in 1971. The Austrian drove for the BRM team in 1973 and was recruited by Ferrari for 1974, when he won his first Grand Prix, at Jarama in Spain. He won the 1975 championship, and looked set to repeat the feat in 1976 when he crashed in flames at the Nürburgring and almost died from his burns. Amazingly, he was back before the end of the season and missed the title by a single point. He took the 1977 title for Ferrari and then joined Brabham before retiring in 1979. But he was back in 1982 to win his third world title with McLaren before he retired again in 1985.

*NIKI LAUDA*

### CHRISTIAN LAUTENSCHLAGER
1877–1954

After working for a time in a cycle factory, the German Lautenschlager joined the Daimler Motoren Gesellschaft in 1900, and became foreman-inspector. After serving as riding mechanic in the 1906 Circuit des Ardennes, he was promoted to driver, although Mercedes' team places were generally offered to gentleman amateurs. His victory in the 1908 Grand Prix so shocked the confident French that the Grand Prix was dropped from the racing calendar until 1912. Mercedes made a comeback in 1914, and Lautenschlager's steady, undramatic driving wore down the opposition from the flamboyant George Boillot in his Peugeot to give a historic Mercedes victory on the eve of World War I.

### GUY LIGIER
1930–

Former French rugby player Guy Ligier entered Formula One driving a Cooper-Maserati in 1966. He raced in twelve Grands Prix before deciding to start his own company in 1968 after the death of his business partner Jo Schlesser at the French Grand Prix. All Ligier's cars carried the designation "JS" in memory of Schlesser. The Matra-engined 1971 JS5 was Ligier's first Grand Prix car, designed by Gerard Ducarouge. Jacques Laffite's win in the new JS7 in the 1977 Swedish Grand Prix was the

*GUY LIGIER*

first "all-French" victory – car, engine, and driver – since the start of the modern world championship series in 1950.

### BRIAN LISTER
1926–

In the early 1950s, Brian Lister decided to set up a racing team in Britain to publicize the long-established Lister engineering firm. He recruited Archie Scott-Brown, who was a fast and daring driver despite the handicap of a deformed hand.

Scott-Brown won two races on the Lister prototype's first outing, and a Lister-Bristol won the sports-car race held during the 1954 British Grand Prix meeting. The 1957 Lister-Jaguars won four major sports-car races. However, at the 1958 Sports Car Grand Prix at Spa, Scott-Brown crashed and was killed, prompting Lister to withdraw from motor racing.

### FRANK LOCKHART
1902–1928

American Frank Lockhart won the Indy 500 in a Miller at his first attempt. A talented engineer, Lockhart developed an intercooler for the super-charged Miller engine, and led the 1927 Indy 500 in his Perfect Circle Miller Special until he was eliminated by engine failure after 120 laps. He then set his sights on developing a car to break the land speed record. His car, the streamlined twin-supercharged, twin-engined Stutz Black Hawk, had a total engine capacity of just 3 litres. In April 1928, the Black Hawk reached 327.32 kph (203.45 mph) on its first run and was making a second run at some 350 kph (220 mph) when a tyre exploded and Lockhart somersaulted to his death.

### NIGEL MANSELL
1953–

After a successful decade in karting, Formula Ford, and Formula Three, Briton Nigel Mansell made his Formula

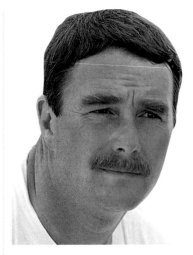

*NIGEL MANSELL*

One debut in 1980 with Lotus. He joined Williams in 1985 and finished second overall in 1986 and 1987. In 1989 he joined Ferrari, but 1991 saw him back with Williams. A record nine victories led to a well-deserved world title in 1992. He stood down from Formula One for 1993 and tried his hand at IndyCar racing in the United States, winning the title for his Newman/Haas team and finishing third in the Indy 500. However, the next year was not so successful and he returned to the Williams Formula One team in mid-season and won one grand prix out of four. He joined McLaren for 1995 before announcing his retirement from Formula One.

### THE MASERATIS

Italian brothers Bindo (b.1883) and Alfieri (1887–1932) Maserati set up a garage in Bologna. In 1922 Alfieri, who had raced before World War I, built a successful special racer powered by one bank of cylinders from an Hispano-Suiza aeroengine. He was then commissioned to build a Grand Prix racer for the Diatto company. When Diatto ran out of money, Alfieri was given the car, which became the first Maserati and won its class in the 1926 Targa Florio. The youngest of the Maserati brothers, Ernesto (1898–1975), successfully raced the new car and, after Alfieri's death in 1932, he joined his brothers Ettore and Bindo in managing the firm. Although the number of cars produced was small, the company enjoyed considerable Grand Prix success.

### RAYMOND MAYS
### 1899–1980

An accomplished sprint and hillclimb driver in the 1920s, Englishman Mays, along with Humphrey Cook and Peter Berthon, conceived the ERA voiturette racer between 1933

*RAYMOND MAYS*

and 1934. After an uncertain start, ERAs enjoyed some success on the racetrack, venturing as far afield as the United States. The cars were built at Mays' home in Bourne, Cambridgeshire. When he could no longer support the

*BRUCE MCLAREN*

venture the factory was shut down and the marque was eventually sold. After World War II, Mays was the moving spirit in the BRM (British Racing Motor) project.

### BRUCE MCLAREN
### 1937–1970

New Zealander Bruce McLaren made his Formula One debut in a Cooper in 1959, when he won the US Grand Prix. He set up his own team in 1964 and by 1968 had fellow New Zealander Denny Hulme driving for him. He won the 1966 Le Mans 24-hour race with Chris Amon, and the 1967 Sebring 12-hour race with Mario Andretti driving Ford GT40s. Maclaren was killed while testing a McLaren Group 7 CanAm racer at Goodwood in 1970.

### HARRY MILLER
### 1875–1943

An intuitive genius with no formal engineering training, Harry Miller was America's leading maker of racing engines in the 1920s and 1930s. With the assistance of machinist Fred Offenhauser, Miller built twin-cam engines which won race after race,

including spectacular victories at Indianapolis. Miller pioneered front-wheel drive with De Dion front suspension in 1924. The Offenhauser engine continued to be the mainstay of American racing until the 1960s.

### STIRLING MOSS
### 1929–

Perhaps Britain's best known racing driver, Stirling Moss was runner-up to the world title four times, but never won a championship. His sports car skills, however, won him the Targa Florio, a legendary Mille Miglia victory, and many other world-class events. Born into a

*STIRLING MOSS*

motoring family, Moss started racing in Formula Three at the age of 18. He moved up to a 996cc Cooper-JAP the following year and was given his first Formula One drive in 1950. He also won the Tourist Trophy in a Jaguar XK120 and became British champion when he won three successive Coupes des Alpes in the Alpine Rally. Moss refused the chance to drive for Ferrari in the early 1950s, on patriotic grounds, but in 1954 he bowed to reality and drove a Maserati to such good effect that he was signed by Mercedes-Benz. The climax of Moss's sports car career was his victory in the 1955 Mille Miglia, when he became the first and only British winner of this race. His passenger, motor racing writer Denis Jenkinson, read lengthy circuit notes out loud to Moss during the race. Their winning time was an all-time record of 157 kph (97 mph). Moss returned to Maserati, winning six Formula One races and six sports car events during 1956. He won the British Grand Prix the following season, and then began driving for Rob Walker's team. An unexplained crash in 1962 prompted him to retire from racing.

### JIMMY MURPHY
### 1894–1924

Starting as a riding mechanic with the Duesenberg team, American Jimmy Murphy was promoted to driver for the 1919 Labor Day meet on the Altoona board track in Pennsylvania. His first victory came later that year when he won the inaugural 250-mile race on the Beverly Hills board track. He was chosen for the Duesenberg team contesting the 1921 French Grand Prix at Le Mans, and gained the first American Grand Prix win. He fitted the winning car with a Miller engine before driving it to victory at Indianapolis in 1922. Murphy's record on the board tracks won him the 1922 US championship. He came second in 1923 and won again in 1924. He was killed in a crash on the Syracuse dirt track in New York.

## FELICE NAZZARO
### 1880–1940

The Italian Felice Nazzaro was an apprentice with Fiat and started racing the new company's cars at the turn of the century. His most

successful year was 1907, when he won all the leading events: the Targa Florio, Grand Prix, and Kaiserpreis. He won the 1913 Targa Florio and Coppa Florio with his own marque of car and retired after the 1914 French Grand Prix. He made a comeback in the 1920s, winning the 1922 French Grand Prix, before retiring again to run Fiat's competition department.

## ALFRED NEUBAUER
### 1891–1980

For 30 years the portly figure of Mercedes team manager "Don Alfredo" Neubauer was a feature of the motor racing scene. He was the first racing team manager to use pit signals as part of a racing plan and to apply team tactics to the winning of races. The German's talents were most on display in the 1930s, when the Mercedes "Silver Arrows" vied for supremacy with the Auto

Unions. When Mercedes returned to motor racing after World War II, Neubauer ensured a formidable tally of wins from 1954 to 1955. But 1955 saw the Le Mans tragedy, when the Mercedes of French driver Levegh hurtled into the grandstand. Neubauer retired and Mercedes withdrew from racing.

## TAZIO NUVOLARI
### 1892–1953

Tazio Nuvolari was a native of Casteldario, near Mantua, Italy, and first made his name as a daring motorcycle racer. He made the transition to four wheels in 1921, driving an Ansaldo, and then raced a 1.5-litre Chiribiri in Spain with

*TAZIO NUVOLARI*

some success. In 1927 he set up a racing team of Bugattis and won five races, but from 1929 he was seen increasingly at the wheel of Alfa Romeos. His first major victory with the marque was the 1930 Mille Miglia, in a 6C1750. Among his other Alfa successes were the 1931 Targa Florio and Coppa Florio and, in 1933, victory at Le Mans and a second Mille Miglia. In 1935

he won eight races with the Alfa "P3", including an epic victory over the might of Mercedes and Auto Union in the German Grand Prix. After a successful 1936 season, he had only one major victory in 1937, and he switched to the Type D Auto Union for 1938. He was one of the very few men who could drive this tricky rear-engined car to the limit. Illness clouded his career after World War II.

## FRED OFFENHAUSER
### 1888–1973

American engineer Fred Offenhauser turned Harry Miller's designs into race-winning cars, and continued the tradition after Miller went bankrupt in 1933. The four-cylinder Offenhauser engine (the "Offy") dominated US racing for the next 40 years, until a change in the rules brought the reign of the Offy to an end in the 1980s. Offenhauser sold the business in 1945, but kept links with racing after his retirement.

## BERNA ELI OLDFIELD
### 1878–1946

Cigar-chomping American cycle racer Berna Eli "Barney" Oldfield became an overnight celebrity when Henry Ford hired him to drive his 18.9-litre racing car "999" in 1902. Oldfield had never driven a car before, but said he would try anything once. He proved to be a natural driver, and barn-stormed around America, promoting the name of Ford. He drove other colourful

*ALFRED NEUBAUER (LEFT)*

*BARNEY OLDFIELD*

racers like the "Winton Bullet" and the "Peerless Green Dragon" in carefully staged exhibition races on local dirt tracks. He also broke speed records on Daytona Beach in the 200-hp Blitzen Benz.

## SIR ALFRED OWEN
### 1893–1975

English businessman Alfred Owen was not particularly interested in motor racing, but he patriotically supported Raymond Mays' British Racing Motors project after World War II. When the original BRM company was wound up at the end of 1952, Owen took over the venture and turned the unreliable V16 BRM into a success. Sir Alfred's faith in the BRM idea was ultimately vindicated when Graham Hill won the 1962 drivers' championship with a new BRM designed by Tony Rudd.

## RALPH DE PALMA
### 1883–1956

Ralph de Palma raced on dirt tracks in the New York area of the United States in 1908, and

raced a Fiat in the Savannah Grand Prize of 1908, finishing ninth. He drove a Simplex in the first Indianapolis 500 in 1911, and the following year led the race from lap three to lap 198, when his 1908 Grand Prix Mercedes broke down. He and his mechanic pushed the car to the finishing line to win eleventh place. He won the Indy 500 only once, with his Grand Prix Mercedes "Gray Ghost" in 1915. De Palma won over 2,000 races in his 25-year career, and set a new land speed record of 240 kph (149 mph) in 1919 with a 14.8-litre Packard V12. He drove in three French Grands Prix in 1912, 1914, and 1921, when he finished second.

## REG PARNELL
### 1911–1964

Briton Reg Parnell started racing in the mid-1930s, but really came to prominence after World War II, racing Maseratis and ERAs with much success. He won at Goodwood so often that he was called "The Emperor of Goodwood". He drove works cars for Alfa Romeo and Aston Martin and won BRM's first victories in 1950. He ended his racing career with victory in the 1957 New Zealand Grand Prix, and went on to run Aston Martin's racing department, guiding them to the 1959 World Sports Car Championship.

## ROGER PENSKE
### 1937–

In his early 20s, Penske was a successful sports car racer, and won the American "D" class

*ROGER PENSKE*

championship three years running from 1961 with the "Zerex Special". Penske won at Laguna Seca and Riverside Raceway in 1962. The American also won the GT class at Sebring the following year in a Ferrari. In 1964 Penske acquired a Philadelphia automobile dealership as the first step in building up a business empire. In 1965 he began team management, and his Penske team have won ten Indianapolis 500 victories to date. Their early success was due to the brilliant driver-engineer Mark Donohue, who won Penske the CanAm championship and the

Indy 500 in 1972. Penske had moved into Formula One in 1971, but Donohue was killed in practice in the 1975 Austrian Grand Prix and was replaced by Ulsterman John Watson. Watson won Penske's only Grand Prix victory in Austria in 1976. Penske pulled out of Formula One racing in 1977.

## NELSON PIQUET
### 1952–

Brazilian-born driver Nelson Piquet won the 1978 British Formula Three championship and was recruited by Brabham for 1979, taking over as team leader when Niki Lauda retired. He won the world title for Brabham in 1981 and 1983, then joined Williams for 1986, winning his third world championship in 1987. A move to Lotus proved unsuccessful, and he joined Benetton for 1990, winning three more Grands Prix before being edged out by the arrival of Michael Schumacher on the team. He left Grand Prix racing and turned his attention to Indianapolis, before retiring through injury.

*NELSON PIQUET*

*ALAIN PROST*

## ALAIN PROST
### 1955–

A graduate of the Paul Ricard Racing School, France's Alain Prost developed his driving skills in karting, in which he was the 1973 world champion, before progressing to cars. He took the French Formula Renault title in 1976 and entered Formula One with McLaren in 1980. He moved to Renault the next season, winning three Grands Prix and finishing second in the championship. He returned to McLaren in 1984 and won three world titles, in 1985, 1986, and 1989, before joining Ferrari for two years. He spent 1992 commentating for French television and made his comeback in 1993 racing for Williams. He won his fourth world championship before retiring in 1994.

## R

## DARIO RESTA
### 1882–1924

Italian-born "Dolly" Resta was a naturalized Briton who began racing at Brooklands in 1907 with a Grand Prix Mercedes. He came second in the 1912 Coupe de l'Auto for Sunbeam, and he set world records at Brooklands the same year with a 3-litre Sunbeam. He went to America in 1914 and won the 1915 Grand Prize and Vanderbilt Cup races with a 1913 Grand Prix Peugeot. He won the Grand Prize and Vanderbilt Cup again in 1916 and also finished second in the Indianapolis 500, becoming America's only foreign National Champion. He retired to please his American wife, but came back to Britain in 1923 and took up racing again, winning the Penya Rhin voiturette race, in Spain, in a Talbot-Darracq. He was killed in a crash in his Sunbeam at Brooklands in 1924.

## DUKE OF RICHMOND AND GORDON (FREDERICK, EARL OF MARCH) 1904–1989

Frederick Charles Gordon-Lennox, England's 9th Duke of Richmond and Gordon, worked as an apprentice for Bentley, and began racing in 1929. In 1930 he won the Brooklands 800-km (500-mile) race with Sammy Davis in an Austin Seven. He won the 1931 Double-Twelve at Brooklands in an MG, then concentrated on team management and official duties from 1932. After World War II, he created the Goodwood circuit on his Sussex estate.

## JOCHEN RINDT
### 1942–1970

Austrian driver Jochen Rindt dominated Formula Two from late 1966 to the end of 1968, before graduating to Formula One with a Lotus-Ford. He won his first Grand Prix in

*JOCHEN RINDT*

1969 at Watkins Glen, New York State. In the 1970 season Rindt won at Monaco in a Lotus 49, and then followed up with four consecutive Grands Prix in the revolutionary wedge-shaped Gold Leaf Team Lotus 72 to lead the championship. However, Rindt crashed during practice for the Italian Grand Prix at Monza and was killed. He is the only posthumous holder of the world title.

## PEDRO AND RICARDO RODRIGUEZ 1940–1971 AND 1942–1962

The sons of a wealthy Mexican building contractor, the Rodriguez brothers had fast cars and motorcycles from an early age. Pedro was racing a Jaguar XK120 at the age of 15, and by the age of 17 was driving a Ferrari for Luigi Chinetti's North American Racing Team at Sebring. Ricardo, who was already Mexican motorcycle champion, drove a Porsche in the same race. The brothers won the Paris 1,000-km (625-mile) race in 1961 and 1962 with Ferraris. In 1960 Ricardo joined the Ferrari Formula One team. They did not compete in the non-championship 1962 Mexican Grand Prix, so Ricardo drove Rob Walker's Lotus-Climax, but he had a fatal crash. Pedro had many victories, including co-driving the winning Ford GT40 at Le Mans in 1968. His Formula One career began in 1967, when he joined Cooper. He won the 1970 Belgian Grand Prix for BRM but was killed in a Formula Two race in Germany.

## BERND ROSEMEYER
### 1909–1938

The rear-engined Grand Prix Auto Union was the only car that German motorcycle ace Bernd Rosemeyer ever raced. Rosemeyer's experience with motorcycles helped him to control the Auto Unions which were difficult to manoeuvre. After a dramatic second place to the great Rudi Caracciola in the 1935 Eifelrennen at the

*BERND ROSEMEYER*

Nürburgring, his first major victory came in that year's Masaryk Grand Prix at Brno, Czechoslovakia. Then in 1936 he won the Eifelrennen, three Grands Prix, and the Coppa Acerbo to take the German championship. The next year showed Rosemeyer at the peak of his abilities, as he held off the challenge of the new W125 Mercedes to win the Eifelrennen, the Vanderbilt Cup, the Coppa Acerbo, and the Donington Grand Prix. In January 1938 he crashed at well over 320 kph (200 mph) during a record attempt on an autobahn and was killed instantly.

## S

## MICHAEL SCHUMACHER
### 1969–

Twice world champion, Michael Schumacher – the first German driver to win the title – came to Formula One in 1991 after a brilliant Formula Three career. At first he signed for Jordan, but after one brilliant race at Spa, Belgium he was recruited by Benetton. In 1992, his car was theoretically outclassed by the Williams-Renaults, but he managed to finish in the top three eight times that season.
His title in 1994

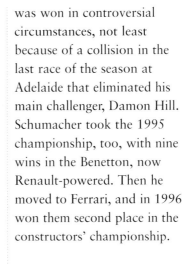

*MICHAEL SCHUMACHER*

was won in controversial circumstances, not least because of a collision in the last race of the season at Adelaide that eliminated his main challenger, Damon Hill. Schumacher took the 1995 championship, too, with nine wins in the Benetton, now Renault-powered. Then he moved to Ferrari, and in 1996 won them second place in the constructors' championship.

## DICK SEAMAN
### 1913–1939

Richard "Dick" John Beattie-Seaman's motor racing career began with an MG Magnette in which he won the 1934 Prix de Berne, Switzerland. He decided to make motor racing his career, despite opposition from his father. He bought an MG Magnette from his friend Whitney Straight, a wealthy American racer, and began racing as a semi-professional. He took it to Switzerland and won the Prix de Berne race. His next acquisition, a 1.5-litre ERA, proved mechanically unreliable. Advised by the great racing mechanic Giulio Ramponi, Seaman bought Earl Howe's 1927 Grand Prix Delage which, prepared by Ramponi, thrashed the more modern ERAs, winning four races out of six in 1936. Seaman also won the British Empire Trophy at Donington in a Maserati and the Donington Grand Prix in an Alfa Romeo.

*DICK SEAMAN*

Seaman joined the Mercedes works team for 1937; his greatest feat was winning the 1938 German Grand Prix at the Nürburgring. He continued to race for Germany in 1939, and was leading in the Belgian Grand Prix at Spa when his car skidded on the wet track and crashed, killing him.

## SIR HENRY SEGRAVE
### 1896–1930

Gallant and charming, Sir Henry Segrave was the first Briton to win an international Grand Prix; in France in 1923. He was also the first man to travel at over 320 kph (200 mph) on land, driving the huge 1000-hp Sunbeam at Daytona, USA, in 1927. In March 1929 Segrave raised the land speed record to 372.46 kph (231.44 mph) driving a car called the "Golden Arrow" at Daytona Beach. Segrave was knighted for his services to national prestige, and his feats made motor racing a popular sport in Britain for the first time. Segrave was killed during his attempt to break the water speed record in 1930.

## AYRTON SENNA
### 1960–1994

Brazilian driver Ayrton Senna started karting at the very early age of four and, by the time he came to Britain in 1981, had won three Kart championship titles in his native Brazil plus two South American championships. He added the British Formula Ford 1600 title to that tally in his first season and in 1982 took the British and European Formula Ford 2000 titles. The next season he won the British Formula Three championship. He was signed for the Formula One Toleman team for 1984 and finished ninth overall in the championship. He then moved to Lotus for 1985, scoring two wins and shifting up to fourth place in the world championship. In 1988 he won the first of three titles for the McLaren marque, before signing for Williams-Renault for 1994; but this potentially unbeatable partnership was cut short in the third race of the season, the San Marino

Grand Prix at Imola, in which he crashed into a wall and was killed. Senna's death ended a career in which he won more than a quarter of the 161 Grands Prix he had contested.

## WILBUR SHAW
### 1903–1954

After three seasons on the dirt tracks, the American Wilbur Shaw raced at Indianapolis for the first time in 1927, finishing fourth. He took second place in 1933 and 1935, before winning in 1937 with his self-built Gilmore-Offy at a record 180 kph (113 mph). He won two Indys in a row in 1939 and 1940 with the Boyle Special, a 3-litre straight-eight Maserati. After the war, Shaw persuaded Tony Hulman to take over the Indianapolis Motor Speedway and served as its president and general manager until his death in a plane crash in 1954.

## CARROLL SHELBY
### 1923–

"Ol' Shel" was a well known and successful American racing driver, familiar to many in his trademark striped bib overalls. He met John Wyer of Aston Martin while racing with an all-American team in the 1954 Argentine 1,000-km race. Soon afterwards he began to race for Aston Martin in England. The high point of Shelby's career was to achieve Aston Martin's only Le Mans victory, when he drove the Aston Martin DBR1/300 with Roy Salvadori. He then retired from racing to concentrate on his V8 Ford-engined AC Cobra venture.

*CARROLL SHELBY*

## JACKIE STEWART
### 1939–

Scotsman Jackie Stewart's early showing in sports car events revealed his natural talent as a racing driver. He quickly graduated to single-seater racing, winning all but two of the Formula Two races he entered in 1964 with Ken Tyrrell's Cooper F3 BMC. He was signed for BRM in 1965, and won the Italian Grand Prix and the Silverstone International Trophy in a BRM V8. He won only one race in the 1966 championship, but compensated with victory in the Tasman Championship. At the end of 1967 he switched from BRM to Ken Tyrrell's Matra team, having already

*JACKIE STEWART*

achieved much with a Matra-Ford in Formula Two. Stewart enjoyed two highly successful seasons. He was championship runner-up in 1968, and in 1969 he secured the Formula One title at the Italian Grand Prix at Monza. Tyrrell tried the new March in 1970, but Stewart won only two races with this car before Tyrrell was back with Matra. He won the championship for Tyrrell in 1971 and 1973 and retired after his 99th Grand Prix, the 1973 US Grand Prix at Watkins Glen. In 1997 he returned to Formula One with the Stewart-Ford team, which he runs with his son Paul.

## JOHN SURTEES
### 1934–

The Briton John Surtees is the only man to have held world titles on both two and four wheels. He began motor racing in 1959, and joined the Formula One Cooper team for 1961, taking second place in the German Grand Prix. His achievements with a Formula One Lola in 1962 earned him a place in the Ferrari works team for 1963, and he won the championship in 1964. Surtees also helped to develop the Lola T70 CanAm sports-racer. He was recovering from a serious accident when he drove a Ferrari 330P/3 to win the 1965 Nürburgring 1,000-km (625-mile) race. He spent the next two seasons working on Honda's new Grand Prix car. He joined BRM for 1969, then founded his own team, which lasted until 1978 and for which he drove until his retirement in 1972.

*AYRTON SENNA*

## FERENC SZISZ
### 1873–1970

One of the few Hungarians to make his name in motor sport, Ferenc Szisz drove the winning Renault in the 1906 French Grand Prix. That first Grand Prix took place over two days, with a total length of 1,240 km

*FERENC SZISZ*

(770 miles), and Szisz averaged a remarkable 98.7 kph (61.3 mph) inclusive of pitstops. He finished second in the 1907 Grand Prix and third in 1908. He drove an Alda in the 1914 French Grand Prix but only came 17th and concluded his career a few weeks later with victory in the Circuit of Anjou in a 12-litre Lorraine-Dietrich.

## T

## RON TAURANAC
### 1925–

Though born in England, Ron Tauranac grew up in Australia and began motor racing with a Formula Three Ralt that he had built with his brother and raced against his friend, the driver Jack Brabham. When

Brabham came to England and established his own company in 1961, he invited Tauranac to join him. Together, the pair founded Motor Racing Developments (MRD) and built the Brabham racing cars. Tauranac designed the space-frame chassis for the 1962 Brabham and MRD eventually took over the running of all Brabham's Formula One activities, with Tauranac as chassis designer. Tauranac sold MRD to Bernie Ecclestone at the end of 1971, and then went back to his racing roots, reviving the Ralt name for a new range of highly successful Formula Two and Formula Three racers.

*KEN TYRRELL*

## KEN TYRRELL
### 1924–

Englishman Ken Tyrrell gave up racing in favour of team management in 1958 and at first ran a Formula Two Cooper team. Tyrrell moved into Formula Junior and in 1964 gave Jackie Stewart his first chance in Formula Three when he won the championship. Tyrrell moved into Formula One for 1968, providing Ford-Cosworth DFV engines for the Matra MS10s that he ran. It was a brilliant move: Stewart was runner-up to the 1968 Formula One title and won the championship in 1969. Matra then wanted to use their own V12 engine, so Tyrrell began to develop his own Formula One chassis. This won the constructors' championship in its first full season, 1971. A later innovation was the Tyrrell six-wheeler which won the 1976 Swedish Grand Prix. By the time Ken Tyrrell retired in the 1990s, his team had contested 416 Grands Prix and won 23.

## U

## AL UNSER AND AL UNSER JR
### 1939– AND 1962–

Four times Indianapolis winner, the American Al Unser won the 500 in 1970, 1971, 1978, and 1987. He also took the US National Championship in 1970, 1983, and 1985. His son, Al Unser Jr, has won the Indianapolis 500 twice, and was also runner-up to his father in the 1985 IndyCar championship – the first time that a father and son had finished a racing series in this position. They were separated by one point. Al Jr went on to win the 1990 and 1994 CART championships.

*AL UNSER*

## V

### TONY VANDERVELL
### 1899–1967

As a young man in the 1920s, British Tony Vandervell drove an aged Talbot and competed at Brooklands. Having left his family's electrical firm in 1926, Vandervell acquired the agency for the new "Thin Wall" replaceable engine bearings that had just been invented in the United States, and built up a highly successful business. After World War II, he was briefly involved with the British Racing Motors (BRM) project before going on to establish his own team. Its first car was a 1949 1.5-litre supercharged Ferrari which was fitted with Vandervell bearings and raced as the "Thin Wall Special". In the early 1950s Vandervell started to develop his own Vanwall racing cars for the new 2.5-litre formula. With Tony Brooks and Stirling Moss driving, the Vanwalls won the 1958 constructors' world championship. However, the team was disbanded at the end of that season due to Vandervell's failing health.

### ACHILLE VARZI
### 1904–1948

Achille Varzi had a racing rivalry with fellow Italian Tazio Nuvolari which lasted throughout the 1930s. They began with T35 Bugattis before moving over to Alfa Romeos. Varzi, driving a 1750 Alfa Romeo, was beaten by Nuvolari in the 1930 Mille Miglia, but entered a road-equipped P2 racer for the

*ACHILLE VARZI*

Targa Florio, and won. He won the Italian championship in 1930, driving Maseratis. He won only one Grand Prix in 1931, driving a Bugatti T51, but had a better year in 1932 with a 4.9-litre T54 Bugatti. This included winning a classic duel against Nuvolari's Alfa Romeo in the Monaco Grand Prix. In 1934, Varzi drove an Alfa Romeo, and won nine races. He won the Tripoli Grand Prix in 1936 in an Auto Union, but lost the Italian Grand Prix to Nuvolari. Varzi was killed in an Alfa 158 during practice for the 1948 Swiss Grand Prix.

### GILLES VILLENEUVE
### 1950–1982

French-Canadian Gilles Villeneuve was a successful Formula Atlantic racer before his first appearance in a Formula One race at the 1977 British Grand Prix. Ferrari signed him to replace Niki Lauda for 1978, and his first

Grand Prix victory was on his home ground in that year's Canadian Grand Prix. He came second in the world championship in 1979 to team-mate Jody Scheckter. He then had two lean years in outclassed cars. In 1982 at the San Marino Grand Prix he came second to Ferrari team-mate Didier Pironi who overtook him on the last lap. Ferrari team orders had been to maintain position, and Villeneuve was furious. In the next Grand Prix in Belgium Villeneuve crashed attempting to beat Pironi's practice lap time and was killed.

### JACQUES VILLENEUVE
### 1971–

Having developed his talents in the Italian and Japanese Formula Three series, Gilles Villeneuve's son Jacques became the youngest-ever American champion in 1994. He went on to win the

Indy 500 in 1995. He test-drove a Williams in 1995, and in his first Formula One season in 1996 he won four Grands Prix to finish second in the world championship. He achieved seven Grand Prix victories the following year to win the 1997 title, also gaining the constructors' championship for Williams for the second year in succession.

## W

### ROB WALKER
### 1917–

Englishman Rob Walker was taken to the Boulogne sports car Grand Prix at the age of seven, and became fascinated by motor racing. While he was at Cambridge University he bought the Delahaye 135 that had belonged to Prince Bira. He raced the car at Brooklands and Le Mans before World War II, and again at Le Mans when the war was over. He then raced Delage and Connaught single-seaters, before making the transition from driver to team owner. In 1958 Stirling Moss drove Walker's Cooper-Climax,

*GILLES VILLENEUVE*

and gained the first Grand Prix victory for a rear-engined car in the modern championship. It was also the first Grand Prix win for a private team. The next year, at Monaco, Moss gained Lotus's first Grand Prix win in Walker's Lotus 18. After Moss's retirement in 1962, Walker employed a succession of great drivers such as Maurice Trintignant, Ricardo Rodriguez, Jo Bonnier, and "Seppi" Siffert. Siffert won the Walker team's last victory, in the 1968 British Grand Prix, driving a new Lotus 49B. It was the last time a private entrant won a Grand Prix.

*ROB WALKER AND JO BONNIER*

### FRANK WILLIAMS
### 1942–

Britain's Frank Williams began buying and selling racing cars in 1967 and by 1968 was running a Formula Two racer for driver Piers Courage. The following year, Williams entered Courage in Formula One in a Brabham. He won the Monaco and US Grands Prix. However, Courage was killed at Zandvoort in 1970, and for the next few years Williams ran his team on very little money. The first Williams car was built in 1972, but the first real success came in 1979 with the Williams FW09. Clay

*FRANK WILLIAMS*

Regazzoni drove the car to victory in the 1979 British Grand Prix at Silverstone, and Williams then won the constructors' championship in 1980 and 1981. Frank Williams was paralysed in a car crash in 1986, but his team won that year's constructors' championship and repeated the feat in 1987. In the 1990s, Williams have won the constructors' championship five times, and the marque's drivers have included Nelson Piquet, Nigel Mansell, Alain Prost, Ayrton Senna, and Damon Hill.

### JEAN-PIERRE WIMILLE
### 1908–1949

The French driver Jean-Pierre Wimille's racing career began with a T51 Bugatti in the 1930 French Grand Prix at Pau, and his first major win was in the 1932 Oran Grand Prix in North Africa. He won the 1936 French sports car Grand Prix at Montlhéry with a Bugatti T57G "Tank", and won the 1937 Le Mans in another T57G. After World War II he switched allegiance to Alfa Romeo and won

consistently from 1946 to 1948. He went to Argentina at the start of the 1949 season with a Simca-Gordini and was killed while practising for the Buenos Aires Grand Prix.

### JOHN WYER
### 1909–1989

Englishman John Wyer began his career as an apprentice at Sunbeam in the 1920s. After World War II he was general manager of Monaco Motors, where he prepared the team of three lightweight HRGs for the 1949 Le Mans and Spa 24-hour races. In 1950 he joined Aston Martin as racing director, and crowned his career with victory at Le Mans in 1959. In 1963 he joined Ford and was responsible for the GT40's 1966 and 1967 Le Mans wins. Ford pulled out of racing the GT40, and JW Automotive, headed by John Wyer and John Willment, took over the project. Two more Le Mans victories followed, then JW made an alliance with Porsche, resulting in the Gulf-Porsche team. The 3-litre Cosworth-engined Gulf-Mirage which won Le Mans in 1975 was Wyer's swansong.

### COUNT LOUIS
### ZBOROWSKI
### 1895–1924

The English-born Polish-American Count Louis Zborowski had a country estate at Higham, in Kent, and built a series of aeroengined racing cars which went under the name of "Chitty-Chitty-Bang-Bang". The first had a 23-litre Maybach six-cylinder aeroengine, and won its first race at Brooklands at over 160 kph (100 mph). It was then raced successfully for two more seasons before being replaced by a touring version with an 18.9-litre Benz engine. Chitty III started as a 7.4-litre Targa Florio Mercedes, but was later fitted with a 14.7-litre Mercedes aeroengine. Like his father who died in 1903 in a Mercedes crash, the Count was killed racing a 2-litre Mercedes at Monza.

*COUNT LOUIS ZBOROWSKI WITH SAMMY DAVIS*

# Glossary

**A-FRAME**

Chassis component, usually a suspension linkage, formed in the shape of a letter "A" for accurate location.

**ACTIVE SUSPENSION**

Suspension that reacts to changing vehicle weight or road conditions to maintain optimum roadholding.

**AEROENGINE**

Power unit, generally of large capacity, originally designed for an aircraft.

**AEROFOILS**

Device of aerodynamic section that generates lift when placed in a moving airstream.

**BRAKES**

Retarding agents on the wheels or, on early cars, the transmission shaft, that were originally drum-shaped with expanding or contracting friction-lined shoes. Now universally disc-type, in which friction-faced pads grip metal or carbon discs that are better able to cope with high temperatures.

**CAMSHAFT**

Shaft with cams (eccentric lobes) mounted on it to operate engine valve gear.

**CARBURETTOR**

Device that mixes fuel and air proportionally. Now generally superseded by fuel injection.

**CHAIN DRIVE**

Transmission system in which the rear wheels carry sprockets driven by chain, usually from driving sprockets on a gearbox output shaft.

**CHASSIS**

The main structural component of a motor car, traditionally a strong channel or box section frame, though some of the very earliest cars had wooden chassis that were strengthened by metal "flitch-plates". Tubular spaceframes were developed later; today's racing cars have strong monocoque chassis, usually formed from carbon fibre.

**CHICANE**

Tight S-bend introduced into a race circuit to reduce competitors' speed, either as a form of handicapping or for safety reasons.

**COIL AND WISHBONE**

Widely used method of independent suspension using A-shaped suspension units ("wishbones") and spiral ("coil") springs.

**COUPLING**

Linkage between two mechanical components, typically two rotating components, often allowing some flexibility.

**COWLING**

Metal or fabric shield, usually to deflect or contain moving air, water, or oil.

**CRABTRACK**

Having a rear axle of narrower track than the front, to improve handling.

**DAMPER**

Device attached to the suspension to control bouncing movement.

**DFV**

"Double Four-Valve" – nomenclature for the Ford-Cosworth Grand Prix engine.

**DOG CLUTCH**

Method of linking two revolving components mechanically using intermeshing toothed couplings.

**DRAG LINK**

Rod linking drop arm to steering arm.

**DROP ARM**

Vertical arm linking the output shaft of a steering box to the drag link, which it moves to and fro to turn the front wheels.

**DUMBIRONS**

Extension of a ladder-type car frame to which suspension leafsprings are attached.

**ERA**

"English Racing Automobiles" – successful racing voiturette of the 1930s.

**EXHAUST**

Means of removing burnt gases from the engine. Exhaust pipes can be "tuned" like musical instruments to increase the rate of flow of the waste gases, thus increasing engine efficiency.

**FAIRING**

Metal or plastic cover that enhances aerodynamic efficiency.

**FORCED INDUCTION**

Compression of the fuel/air mixture going into the engine allowing more fuel to be burned, increasing power.

**FUEL-INJECTION**

System in which fuel charges into the engine are positively metered, either mechanically or electronically, to give precise control of combustion.

**GROUND-EFFECT**

Using the aerodynamic interference between the car and the track surface to generate negative lift and increase cornering speeds.

**GURNEY STRAP**

Thin strip of carbon fibre on the trailing edge of an aerofoil that increases downforce.

**HORSEPOWER**

Unit used to define the power output of an engine, usually expressed as developed or "brake" horsepower ("bhp").

**INLINE FOUR**

Engine with four cylinders in a line.

**KEVLAR**

Type of carbon fibre sheeting used in monocoque chassis construction.

**LATTICE GIRDER**

Light but strong construction using two parallel bars linked by interlaced crossbracing.

**LAYDOWN ROADSTER**

Called roadsters from their low seating position, these oval-track racers had the engine laid almost horizontal as far to the left as possible to shift weight to the inside of the turns.

**LEAFSPRING**

The earliest type of suspension spring, made up of laminated strips of spring steel.

**MAINPLANE**

The principal surface of a car's wing.

**MALITE**

Aluminium sheeting, sandwiching a balsa wood

core, used in chassis construction.

## MONOCOQUE

From the French, literally meaning "single shell" – a method of chassisless construction.

## MONOPOSTO

From the Italian, literally meaning "single-seater".

## NACA DUCT

Intake system developed by the American aerospace industry and applied to cars. It uses airflow over a car's surface to force air down a constantly-narrowing aperture.

## NART

"North American Racing Team" run by American Ferrari agent Luigi Chinetti.

## PLENUM

Chamber into which air is drawn to keep fuel injection units supplied.

## PUSH ROD

Rod pushing against rocker to open overhead valves, or against inboard springing unit as part of the suspension system.

## RADIUS ROD

Suspension component pivoted on the chassis at its forward end to locate road wheels or axles.

## RAIL FRAME

Ladder-type chassis with channel girder side members.

## RAJO OVERHEAD VALVE CONVERSION

Proprietary cylinder head fitted to convert Model T Ford from side to overhead valve operation to increase efficiency.

## RIDE-HEIGHT ADJUSTERS

Device used to vary the ground clearance of a car in the search for cornering efficiency.

## ROLL BAR

Transversely-mounted suspension component connected to front or rear suspension links to limit body roll during cornering.

## SERVO

An auxiliary device which, on a car, reduces the effort needed to operate brakes or steering (from the Latin "servus", meaning slave).

## SHOCK ABSORBER

See **Damper**

## SIDEVALVES

Cylinder with its valves by its side. Otherwise known as "flat-head" or "L-Head".

## SLEEVE VALVE

An alternative to poppet valves for internal combustion engines using sliding sleeves between cylinder walls and piston which expose the inlet and exhaust ports as they rise and fall. Now obsolete.

## SLIDING SKIRT

Aerodynamic device (now banned) which closes the gap between the car body and track surface in order to generate maximum downforce.

## SPACEFRAME

Light but extremely strong chassis structure of cross-braced or triangulated metal tubes.

## SPORTS TOURER

Sports car with luggage accommodation for at least a sponge bag and toothbrush.

## SPIDER OR "SPYDER"

Open two-seater sports car (originally a light two-wheeled carriage with an exposed seat behind for the "spider" or groom).

## STOCK-BLOCK

Engine using the cylinder block from a production family car.

## STONEGUARD

Wire mesh to prevent flying stones from damaging lamps or radiator.

## SUPERCHARGING

A positively-driven compressor providing forced induction. There are three basic types: vane-type, with sliding vanes mounted on an eccentric rotor to compress the air against the supercharger wall; roots, with two intermeshing rotors compressing the air between them; and centrifugal, with a finned rotor compressing the air as it spins at high speed.

## SUSPENSION

The springing and locating medium used between chassis frame and road wheels.

## SWING-AXLES

Form of independent suspension in which the axle shafts pivot around a fixed final drive unit.

## THIN-WALL BEARING

Replaceable engine bearings, first seen in the 1920s, which gave better heat dissipation than white-metal bearings, allowing engines to run more reliably at higher revolutions.

## TORSION BAR

Metal bar fixed at one end, free to turn at the other,

which provides springing medium by its resistance to twisting forces.

## TRACTION CONTROL

Method of controlling the power fed to the driving wheels to prevent loss of grip through wheelspin – now illegal.

## TRAILING LINK

Suspension component pivoted at its forward end and carrying the wheel hub at its rear end.

## TRANSAXLE

Combined gearbox and final drive unit, often used in conjunction with De Dion axle layout.

## TRANSMISSION

Gearbox and final drive system used to transmit engine power to road wheels.

## TWIN-CAM

Engine with two overhead camshafts.

## VALVES

Devices which act as "doors" to let the gases in and out of the cylinder. Poppet valves are the most common and are shaped like metal mushrooms with long stems.

## VENTURI

Restricted passage which speeds up the flow of gas or liquid.

## VOITURETTE

Racing car of intermediate class, below Grand Prix standard, the forerunner of modern Formula Two.

## ZF

"Zahnrad Fabrik" – German transmission engineering company.

# Index

*Index entries in bold refer to main headings, those in italic refer to illustrations*

# Acknowledgments

I WOULD LIKE to thank the following for their help and advice: Howard R. Davies, Jaguar Daimler Heritage Trust; John Pulford, Brooklands Museum; David Holland, Brooklands Society; Evert Louwman, Het Nationaal Automobielmuseum, Raamsdonksveer, Holland; Ford Motor Company; Indianapolis Motor Speedway; National Automobile Museum, Reno, Nevada; National Motor Museum, Beaulieu, Hampshire; Jacques Potherat, Vintage Montlhéry Lalique; Jonathan Stein, Automobile Quarterly; Richard Sutton, Goodwood Festival of Speed; Joan Williamson and Moira O'Farrell, Royal Automobile Club; Nancy Edwards, TAG McLaren; Richard Smith (1905 Star); Tim Moore (1884 De Dion, Bouton, and Trépardoux); Lindley F. Bothwell Jr (1914 Grand Prix Peugot); Karen Dron, Coy's Historic Festival.

**Photography by:**
Gary Ombler, Richard Shellabear, Steve Gorton, Tom Wood, Dave Rudkin, Dave King, and Matthew Ward

**Dorling Kindersley would like to thank the following:**
Andy Komorowski for photography assistance; Ellen Woodward and Mark Wilde for their idea for the book; Chris Walker for design assistance; the staff at The National Motor Museum, Beaulieu; Anne-Marie Wolf and Jacobi Hoolmans at Het Nationaal Automobielmuseum; Gert Straub and Dieter Ritter at the Mercedes-Benz Museum Collection; Anna Guerrier and Nancy Edwards at TAG McLaren; Tony O'Keeffe and Tony Burton at the Jaguar Daimler Heritage Trust; Ellen Bireley, Donald Davidson, Jan Layden, Barney Wimmer, Jim McKinney, and special thanks to Terry Gunter at the Indianapolis Motor Speedway Foundation.

The Indianapolis car pictures on pages 52-53, 70-71, 92-93, 122-123 are 1998 Copyright Indianapolis Motor Speedway Foundation. All rights Reserved. Used under licence.

**Dorling Kindersley would also like to thank the following for their kind permission to reproduce the photographs:**

a=above; c=centre; b=below; l=left; r=right; t=top;

Allsport: David Taylor 129 crb, Steve Swope 23 tr, Vincent Laforet 128 tr, 129 ca, 129 tr; Automobile Quarterly: 30 clb, 30 bl, 30 -31bc, 31 crb, 31 tr, 31 tl, 35 cr, 46 tl; Henry Ford Museum 100 tr, 100 bl, 101 tr; Vincente Alverez/Bruce Craig Racing Photos 13 tc; Bridgeman Art Library: John Noott Galleries, Broadway, Worcs. 42 bl; Michelin Building, London 12 tc, 37 tl ; © Brooklands Museum 42 cl, 42 tr, 42 -43bc, 43 ca, 43 tl; Neill Bruce Motoring Photolibrary: 36 tr, 50 bc, 51 tr, 54 tr, 55 cr, 61 tr, 63 cra, 74 -75c, 74 bl, 75 cra, 75 cr, 75 crb, 78 tr, 82 clb, 88 tr, 96 bl, 106 cl, 121 cb, 133 br; Car courtesy Brooks Auctioneers 82 crb; Peter Roberts Collection 8 -9, 16 bc, 17 crb, 19 tr, 31 cra, 36 -37cb, 36 bl, 37 cra, 37 br, 61 tl, 100 cl; Bruce Craig Photos: 68 tl, 68 -69c, 68 clb, 68 br, 69 clb, 85 br, 85 crb, 85 cra; David Burgess-Wise: 28 tl, 30 tl, 39 tl, 43 cr, 69 br, 69 tl, 72 bl, 73 bc, 101 cra; Jean-Loup Charmet: 14 clb, 38 tl; Collector's Car Books: BRSCC 102; Corbis UK Ltd: 34 cl, 34-35cb, 35 tl; Bettmann/Agence France Presse 139cr; Bettmann/ Baldwin H. Ward 34 tr; Hulton Getty 82tr; George Lepp 96 cl; Reuters/Bettmann 22 tc, 132 tr, UPI 18 bc, 85 cb, UPI/Bettmann 160 br; Coys Archives Ltd, London: 6, 40, 60 tl; Automobile Club of Monaco 86; Dexter Brown 126, 130 tl; Greg Crisp: 134 bl, 134 cla, 134 tr, 134 -135, 134 br, 135 bc, 135 crb, 135 cra; Daimler-Benz AG: 62-63c, 62 tcr; Daytona Racing Archives: 112-113c, 112-113bc, 112 tl, 112 tr, 113 bc, 113 cra, 113 tr, 113 tl, 113 crb, 135 tr, 135 tl; Dove Publishing: Automobile Club di Milano 88 tl; British Automobile Racing Club 78 tl; Koninklijke Nederlansche Automobiel Club 98tl; RAC 104 tl; Agence DPPI: 108 tr, 109 tr, 109 cra, 110 bcr; E.T. Archive: Museum fur Gestaltung, Zurich 66; V & A 26, 42 tl; Ford Motor Company Ltd: 20 br, 101 cb; Hulton Getty: 32 tr, 34 tl, 35 tr, 44 tr, 61 cr, 72-73c, 73 tr, 130-131c, 131 cr; Empics Ltd 138-139cb, 138 tl, 139 tcl; © Indianapolis Motor Speedway: 52 tr, 70 br, 84-85, 84 ca, 84 tl, 85 tr, 92 tr, 100br, 114, 122 tr, 128-129, 128 tl, 128 ca, 140-141; Elwood Simmons 129 tl; Jim Haines Collection 68 tr, 69 tc, 69 cra, 129 cra; LAT Photographic: 24-25, 73 tl, 76 tr, 82

cla, 97 tl, 97 bc, 98 bl, 104 cl, 104 bc, 104 tr, 104-105, 105 tl, 105 tc, 105 br, 105 tr, 106 tr, 108 bl, 108-109, 108 cb, 108 cl, 109 crb, 109 tl, 109 tc, 110 cla, 116tl, 116tr, 116cl, 116bl, 116-117, 117tl, 117cra, 117ca, 117br, 117bl, 118 tr, 120-121c, 120 bcl, 120 tr, 121 tl, 121 cra, 124 bl, 124 tl, 124 tr, 124 cl, 124-125cb, 125 ca, 125 tr, 125 crb, 125 tl, 130 clb, 130 tr, 131 tr, 131 bc, 131 ca, 131 tl, 136 tr, 138 bl, 138 tr, 139 cra, 139 tr, 139 crb, 157 bcl; Ludvigsen Library: 28-29c, 36 clb, 37 c, 72 tr, 80 tr; Midsummer Book Ltd: 76cl, 76-77bc, 77tcl, 77cla, 77cra; National Motor Museum: 5 tl, 10 c, 11 tr, 11 bc, 15 tr, 16 tc, 28 cl, 28 tr, 29 cr, 29 tr, 29 tl, 30 tr, 36tl, 38 tcr, 38 bl, 38 cl, 38-39c, 39 tr, 39 br, 46br, 46 cl, 46 -47c, 47tl, 47 tr, 48-49cr, 48 br, 48 cl, 48 tl, 48 tr, 48 clb, 49 tr, 49 br, 49 tl, 50 tr, 54 bl, 54cl, 54-55c, 55tc, 55tr, 55br, 58br, 58tr, 58bl, 58cl, 59bl, 59tc, 59tr, 60br, 60bl, 60tr, 60-61c, 62 br, 62 bl, 62 clb, 63 tl, 64 tr, 64 bl, 64-65bc, 64 tl, 65 cla, 65 tr, 74 clb, 78 br, 78-79c, 78 cl, 79 tl, 79 br, 83 tl, 83 tr, 83 cra, 88-89c, 88 cl, 89 tr, 89 tl, 90 clb, 90-91cb, 90 tr, 91 cr, 91 tr, 91 tl, 91 crb, 94-95, 94 tr, 95 crb, 95 tc, 95 c, 95 cra, 95 tcl, 96 tr, 96-97c, 97 tr, 98 cl, 98 tr, 99 tl, 99 tr, 99 cr, 101 tl, 106-107bc, 120 cl, 121 bl, 133 tcl, 142 bcr, 142 cl, 142 tcl, 143 tr, 143 br, 143 tl, 143 bl, 144 bcr, 144 clb, 145 tl, 145 tr, 145 br, 145 bcl, 146 bl, 146 tr, 147 br, 147 tcr, 148 bl, 148 clb, 148 tcr, 148 br, 149 cl, 149 tr, 149 br, 150 tl, 150 bcl, 150 br, 151 tcr, 151 cl, 151 bl, 152 tr, 152 cl, 152 cla, 153 bcr, 153 tc, 153 clb, 154 crb, 154 bl, 155 br, 155 tl, 155 tcr, 156 bl, 156 tl, 157 cla, 157 tr, 158 tcr, 158 bl, 158 bcr, 159 cla, 159 br, 159 crb, 160 tcl, 161 cl, 161 br, 161tcl; ©Automobile Club of Monaco 90 tl; Automobile Club de l'Ouest 20 clb, 94 tl; Pook's Motor Bookshop: V.F1.Zolder/Royal Automobile Club Belgique 108 tl; Porsche AG: 110 tr, 111 tl; Jacques Potherat: 50 cl, 50 tl, 50-51c, 51 tl, 51 cra; Quadrant Picture Library: 72 bcr, 74 crb, 74 tcr, 75 tl, Autocar 78 clb; William Taylor: 97 cra; Temple Press Ltd: 72tl; Topham Picturepoint: 22-23bc, 28 bl, 34 bl, 69 crb, 72 cl, 83 crb, 94 clb, 98-99cb, 121 tr, 127 bc, 132 bl, 132 cl, 133 tr.

Jacket: David Burgess-Wise: inside back t; LAT Photographic: front bc; Jeff Bloxham front cl; National Motor Museum: inside front cb, back cb.

For Matthew
~ CL

For Sven
~ GH

This edition produced for The Book People Ltd
Hall Wood Avenue, Haydock, St Helens WA11 9UL, by
LITTLE TIGER PRESS
1 The Coda Centre, 189 Munster Road, London SW6 6AW

First published in Great Britain 2003

Printed in Singapore • ISBN 1 85430 853 X
1 3 5 7 9 10 8 6 4 2

# MOLLY and the STORM

## Christine Leeson  Gaby Hansen

TED SMART

It was the first sunny day after weeks and weeks of rain.

"Can we go out to play, Mum?" asked Molly Mouse, dancing in the pale sunshine. "Please?"

"So long as you keep an eye on the weather," said Mother Mouse. "I'm sure more rain is on the way."

Molly and her brothers
and sister scampered across the fields.
They chased each other round hawthorn trees,
frothing white with blossom.

They hopped through
carpets of bluebells.

They were enjoying themselves
so much that they didn't notice
it was suddenly getting darker.

PLOP!
A large drop of rain fell on Molly's
nose – and another, and then another.
Big black clouds filled the sky, and
the rain started to fall faster and faster.
"We'll never get home in time," groaned
Molly. "Where can we shelter until it stops?"

Just then, a squirrel hurried by on her
way home. She stopped when she saw
the wet little mice. Her own family were
all tucked up safe and warm in her nest.
She couldn't possibly leave the mice
out in the rain.

"Come with me," she said.
"You can shelter at my place."

Squirrel ran ahead and bounded
up a tree, but the mice didn't follow.
"Your house is too high and it doesn't
look safe in this storm," sighed Molly.

An old harvest mouse popped
her head out from under some leaves.
"You can stay with me," she said kindly,
"I have a nice warm nest of twigs."

Harvest Mouse scuttled to her home, but the mice didn't follow. They could see that her woven nest was far too small for them all.

"You can come to our place," cried a little rabbit, "and join my baby brothers and sisters in the warmth of our burrow." She couldn't leave these poor little mice out in the storm.

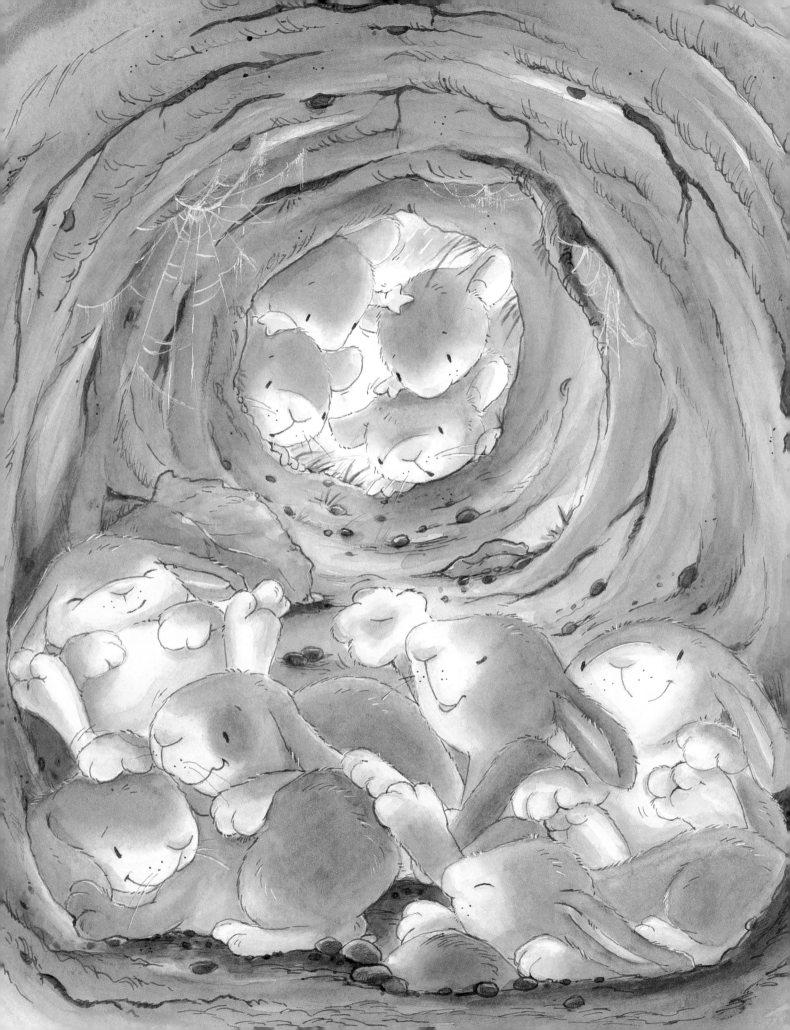

Rabbit popped down the rabbit hole, but the mice stayed outside. "Your home is very full," said Molly, peering inside at all the baby rabbits. "I think we'd all be too squashed."

Before Rabbit had time to answer, they both heard someone calling. Molly pricked her ears. "It's Mother Mouse!" she squeaked.

"Thank goodness I've found you!" cried Mother Mouse. "The storm is getting worse. But there's an old hollow oak tree near by where we can shelter until the rain stops."

The hollow oak tree stood at the top of a slope. The mice scrambled inside and were soon warm and dry.
"We'll stay here tonight," said Mother Mouse. "You can all curl up together and go to sleep."

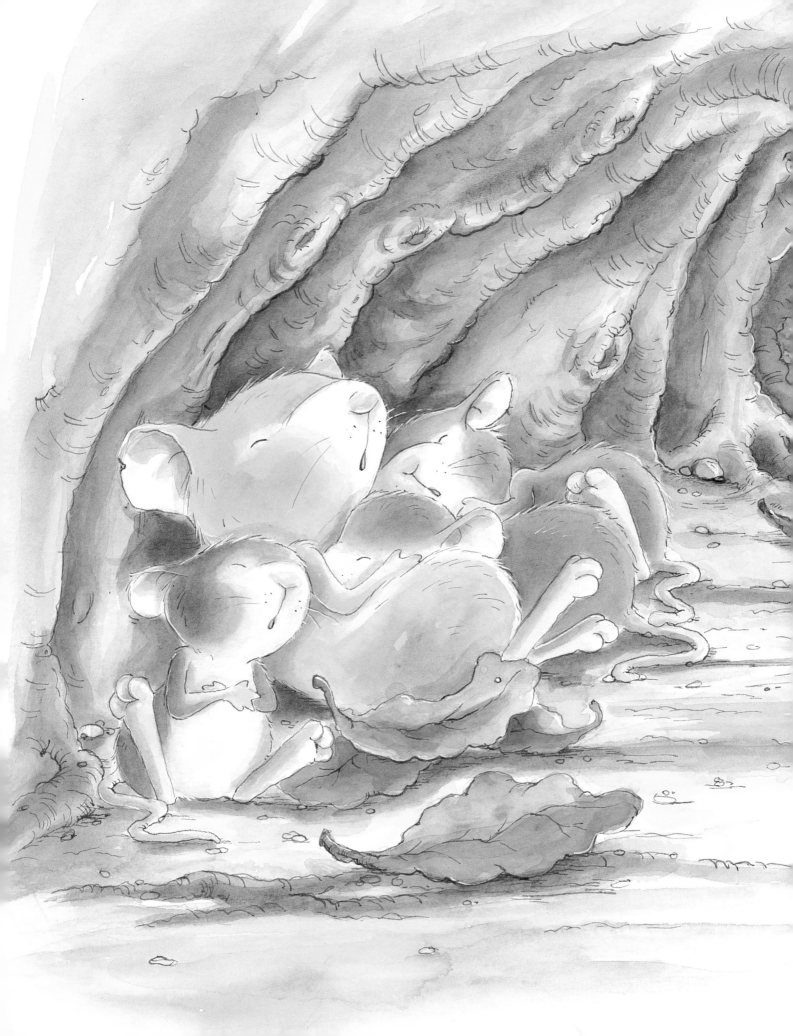

But Molly couldn't sleep. She lay listening to
the roar of the wind and the lashing of the rain,
and she was worried about her new friends.
Would Harvest Mouse's home be destroyed?
Surely Rabbit's burrow would be flooded,
and Squirrel's nest blown away? Molly looked
at her family, sleeping snugly. She couldn't
leave her friends out in the storm.

Molly hurried outside. The wind tugged and
pulled at her as she struggled across the field.
There, huddled under a swaying tree,
was Squirrel.

"You must come with me,"
said Molly. "We've
found the perfect
shelter."

Just then, looking tired and bedraggled, the
old harvest mouse appeared out of the grass.
"Can I come too?" she asked.
"Of course," said Molly.

As they made their way back,
they passed Rabbit and
her family huddled
under a hedge. "You'll
be nice and warm if
you come with us,"
said Molly.

At last Molly and her new friends reached the shelter of the old oak tree. Outside, the wind battered the trees and flattened the grasses. But inside, everyone was safe and dry.

The wind had dropped by the time morning came, and as the sun crept up into the sky the friends crawled out of their burrow. There before them was a rainbow, stretching as far as the eye could see.

"It's for you, Molly," whispered the old harvest mouse. "It's a special present for saving us."
And Molly smiled happily, surrounded by her family and all her new friends.